Knit Your Own
Kama Sutra

Twelve Playful Projects for Naughty Knitters

HarperCollins books may be purchased for educational, business,
or sales promotional use. For information, please e-mail the Special
Markets Department at SPsales@harpercollins.com.

Published in 2014 by:
Harper Design
An Imprint of HarperCollins*Publishers*
195 Broadway
New York, NY 10007
Tel: (212) 207-7000
Fax: (212) 207-7654
harperdesign@harpercollins.com
www.harpercollins.com

Distributed throughout the world by
HarperCollins*Publishers*
195 Broadway
New York, NY 10007

Commissioning Editor: Jacqueline Ford
Assistant Editor: Tamsin Richardson
Editor: Claire Crompton
Art Director: Lucy Smith
Layout: Michelle Rowlandson
Cover design: Lucy Smith
Artworker & Prop Design: Rebecca Hawkins
Photography: Volfgang Knipsen
Illustrations: Rob Brandt

Library of Congress Control Number: 2014940260

ISBN 978-0-06-235200-2

Printed in China

First Printing, 2015

Knit Your Own
Kama Sutra

Twelve Playful Projects for Naughty Knitters

Trixie von Purl

Harper DESIGN

An Imprint of HarperCollins Publishers

Contents

HOW TO USE THIS BOOK

The knitted *Kama Sutra*—where has it been all your life, you ask yourself?! I often struggle when I try to describe to people what I do for a living, and this book hasn't made it any easier. What I do know is that bringing these creations to life has been a joy, and I hope you have as much fun yourselves coming up with your own cast of naughty and adventurous knitted characters.

Knit Your Own Kama Sutra is not your average knitted doll book; for a start there is a lot of detail involved in the designs, including the dolls themselves, which means that close attention needs to be paid to the patterns. Most of the projects are knitted using fingering/4ply yarn and fine needles (US size 2 to 5), and the dolls themselves are knitted in rounds on 4 or 5 double pointed needles. Although there are plenty of simple, straightforward designs contained in these pages, many of them might not be appropriate for complete beginners. I'm a firm believer in putting a bit of extra effort into my creations, and hopefully you'll agree with me that the extra detailing takes the dolls and their accessories to another level. If you're in doubt about their complexity, check out the Abbreviations (p. 108) and Basic Techniques (pp. 16–17) sections.

Much of the fun to be had comes at the hair and facial features stage—often I'd have an idea of how I wanted the character to look, only to find they had ideas of their own. The doll patterns are the same throughout, but it's amazing how varied you can make them look by using different hairstyles, yarn color choices, facial features, and even the amount of stuffing you put into them! The techniques used are similar for both male and female dolls (with the obvious shaping differences), but different needle sizes are used, which means the male dolls are slightly larger than the females. You can, of course, make them the same size by adjusting the needle size, but please bear that in mind when it comes to knitting any accompanying garments, and alter the needle sizes for those as well.

On pages 8–15 you'll find the basic doll patterns, plus information about some of the other techniques used, but below are a couple of general pointers.

YARN

Each pattern has a Materials section which gives yarn suggestions—and suggestions is exactly what they are. Feel free to experiment with your own yarns as these projects make ideal stash-busters, but make sure you use something the same weight (or thickness) as the original. If the pattern suggests a fingering/4ply yarn, stick to that yarn thickness. Some projects use a very small amount of one particular color that doesn't necessitate buying a whole ball, in which case the pattern will read "Small amount of xxx yarn," and hopefully your stash will provide.

Most of the patterns have a gauge guide. If this were a life-size garment book I'd tell you to stick rigidly to this and always knit a gauge swatch, but here we can afford to be a little more relaxed—the items are small so any differences in gauge won't be quite so obvious in the finished outcome. Where there is no gauge guide, the finished size is negligible.

STRUCTURES

Some of the items use cardboard as an interior structure to support the knitting (for instance, the photocopier and suitcase). The deck chairs even require some simple woodwork. Where there is a shape involved I have included a template for you to copy, whereas the simpler patterns will give you the dimensions to work to. All of the materials required are easy to find, either around the home or from craft and hardware stores.

So off you go, you naughty knitters, and, above all, have fun!

MATERIALS

- Yarn in the following options:
- 1 x 50g ball Debbie Bliss Rialto 4ply (fingering 100% wool; 50g/196yds) in shade 034 Blush OR shade 038 Mink

OR

- 1 x 50g ball King Cole Merino Blend 4ply (fingering 100% wool; 50g/196yds) in shade 790 Caramel OR shade 929 Fudge
- Small amounts of yarn in preferred color for hair, eyes, and mouth
- Set of 5 x US 2 dpns
- 6 stitch holders
- 8 pipe cleaners 12" long x ¼" thick

GAUGE

Approx 30 sts and 48 rows = 4" over St-st.

FINISHED MEASUREMENTS

Approx 11 ½" from head to heel.

NOTE: The doll is knitted in rnds from the toes up. The arms and legs are made separately using 4 dpns and then joined into the torso as it is worked on 5 dpns. Stuff the doll and add pipe cleaners where indicated (see p. 16 for stuffing tips).

LEG (make 2)
Foot

With 2 dpns, cast on 3 sts.
Next row: Kfb into each st (6 sts).
Slip 2 sts onto each of 3 dpns. Place a marker at beg of rnd. Work in rnds from now on.
Rnd 1: K.
Rnd 2: (Kfb) 3 times, k2, kfb (10 sts).

Rnd 3: K.
Rnd 4: Kfb, k2, (kfb) twice, k4, kfb (14 sts).
Rnd 5: K.
Rnd 6: Kfb, k4, (kfb) twice, k6, kfb (18 sts).
There should now be 8 sts on needle 1 (sole of foot), and 5 sts each on needles 2 and 3 (foot top).
Rnds 7 to 16: K.

Shape Heel

The heel is worked on 8 sts on needle 1 only (work back and forth instead of in rnds).
Row 1: K7, w&t.
Row 2: P6, w&t.
Row 3: K5, w&t.
Row 4: P4, w&t.
Row 5: K3, w&t.
Row 6: P2, w&t.
Row 7: K3, working wrap into st, turn.
Row 8: P4, turn.
Row 9: K5, turn.
Row 10: P6, turn.
Row 11: K7, turn.
Row 12: P8.

Ankle & Calf

Beg working in rnds again:
Rnd 1: K8 from needle 1, pick up yarn strand lying between last st knitted and next st on needle 2, sl onto needle 2 and k tog with next st (this closes gap between heel and foot). K to end.
Rnd 2: Pick up yarn strand laying between last st knitted and first st on needle 1, sl onto needle 1 and k tog with next st (this closes gap between heel and foot). K to end.
Rnds 3 to 6: K.
Rnd 7: K1, skpo, k2, k2tog, k to end (16 sts).

Rnds 8 to 15: K.
Rnd 16: K2, m1R, k2, m1L, k to end (18 sts).
Rnds 17 and 18: K.
Rnd 19: K1, m1R, k6, m1L, k to end (20 sts).
Rnds 20 to 29: K.

Knee

Rnd 1: K1, skpo, k4, k2tog, k to end (18 sts).
Rnds 2 and 3: K.
Rnd 4: K1, skpo, k2, k2tog, k to end (16 sts).
Rnd 5: K1, skpo, k2tog, k3, m1R, k6, m1L, k2 (16 sts).
Rnd 6: K6, m1R, k8, m1L, k2 (18 sts).
Rnd 7: K6, m1R, k10, m1L, k2 t(20 sts).
Rnds 8 and 9: K.
Rnd 10: K6, skpo, k8, k2tog, k2 (18 sts).
Rnd 11: K1, m1R, k2, m1L, k3, skpo, k6, k2tog, k2 (18 sts).
Rnd 12: K8, skpo, k4, k2tog, k2 (16 sts).

Thigh

Rnd 1: K1, m1R, k4, m1L, k to end (18 sts).
Rnd 2: K1, m1R, k6, m1L, k2, m1R, k8, m1L, k1 (22 sts).
Rnds 3 to 5: K.
Rnd 6: K1, m1R, k8, m1L, k2, m1R, k10, m1L, k1 (26 sts).
Rnds 7 to 11: K.
Rnd 12: K1, m1R, k10, m1L, k2, m1R, k12, m1L, k1 (30 sts).
Rnd 13: K1, m1R, k to end (31 sts).
Rnds 14 to 23: K.
Slip 15 sts from needle 1 onto first st-holder (this will be the back of the leg), 16 sts from needles 2 and 3 onto second st-holder (this will be the front of the leg—see illus 1).

▶

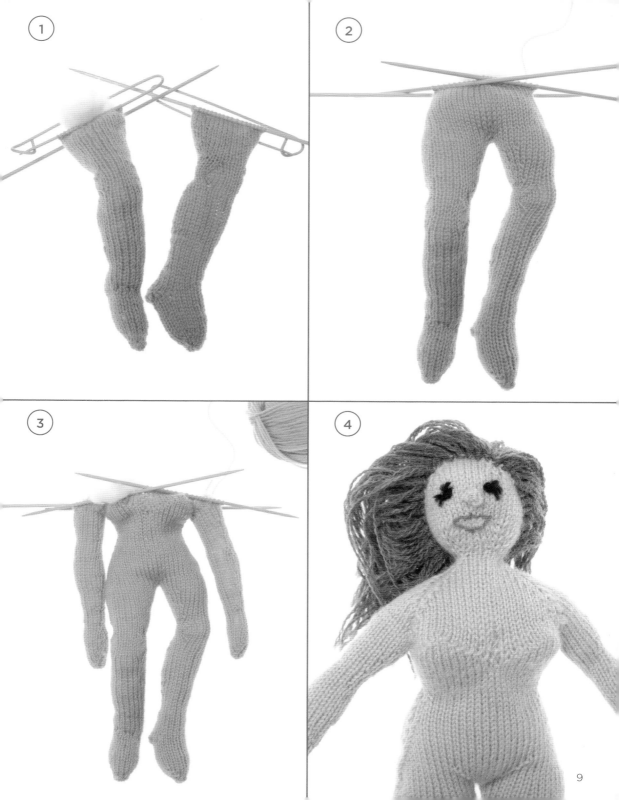

① ② ③ ④

TORSO
Join Legs
Use 4 dpns. With RS facing, slip 16 sts of front of first leg onto needle 1, 16 sts of front of second leg onto needle 2, 15 sts of back of second leg onto needle 3, 15 sts of back of first leg onto needle 4 (62 sts). Place a marker for beg of rnd. Rejoin yarn, k 1 rnd (see illus 2).

Buttocks
Rnd 1: K14, p1, k2, p1, k to end.
Rnd 2: K13, p1, k4, p1, k16, m1R, k9, m1L, k6, m1R, k9, m1L, k3 (66 sts).
Rnd 3: Skpo, k10, p1, k6, p1, k10, k2tog, skpo, k1, m1R, k11, m1L, k2, k2tog, k2, m1R, k11, m1L, k1, k2tog (65 sts).
Rnd 4: K10, p1, k8, p1, k to end.
Rnd 5: Skpo, k7, p1, k10, p1, k7, k2tog, skpo, m1R, k14, m1L, k1, k2tog, m1R, k14, m1L, k2tog (64sts).
Rnd 6: K.
Rnd 7: Skpo, k24, k2tog, skpo, m1R, k14, m1L, k2tog, skpo, m1R, k14, m1L, k2tog (62 sts).
Rnd 8: K.

Shape Waist
Rnd 9: Skpo, k22, k2tog, skpo, k to last 2 sts, k2tog (58 sts).
Rnd 10: K.
Rnd 11: Skpo, k20, k2tog, (skpo) twice, k11, k2tog, skpo, k11, (k2tog) twice (50 sts).
Rnd 12: K.
Rnd 13: Skpo, k18, k2tog, (skpo) twice, k8, k2tog, skpo, k8, (k2tog) twice (42 sts).
Rnd 14: K.
Rnd 15: K22, skpo, k3, k2tog, k4, skpo, k3, k2tog, k2 (38 sts).
Rnd 16: K20, skpo, k14, k2tog (36 sts).
Rnd 17: K21, skpo, k1, k2tog, k4, skpo, k1, k2tog, k1 (32 sts).
Rnd 18: Skpo, k16, k2tog, skpo, k to last 2 sts, k2tog (28 sts).
Rnd 19: K20, m1R, k1, m1L, k4, m1R, k1, m1L, k2 (32 sts).
Rnd 20: K1, m1R, k16, m1L, k2, m1R, k to last st, m1L, k1 (36 sts).
Rnd 21: K24, m1R, k3, m1L, k4, m1R, k3, m1L, k2 (40 sts).
Rnd 22: (K1, m1R, k18, m1L, k1) twice (44 sts).
Rnd 23: K.
Rnd 24: (K1, m1R, k20, m1L, k1) twice (48 sts).
Rnd 25: K.
Rnd 26: (K1, m1R, k22, m1L, k1) twice (52 sts).
Rnd 27: K.
Rnd 28: K1, m1R, k24, m1L, k to end (54 sts).

Shape Breasts
Each is worked separately. The chest sts are divided into two sections of 14 sts each, which are shaped with short rows.
Row 1: K13, w&t.
Row 2: P12, w&t.
Row 3: K11, w&t.
Row 4: P10, w&t.
Row 5: K9, w&t.
Row 6: P8, w&t.
Row 7: K7, w&t.
Row 8: P6, w&t.
Row 9: K5, w&t.
Row 10: P4, w&t.
Row 11: K3, w&t.
Row 12: P2, w&t.
Row 13: K8, turn, working wraps into sts.
Row 14: P14, turn, working wraps into sts.
Cut yarn and rejoin to 14 sts on needle 2 for second breast. Rep rows 1 to 14, ending at center of chest. Cut yarn. With RS facing, rejoin yarn to beg of rnd, k across 28 sts of chest. Cut yarn. With RS facing, rejoin yarn to beg of needle 3, k across 26 sts of back, turn.
Next row: P26, turn.
Next row: K26 to end of row.
Next row: Bind off 2 sts, k24, bind off 4 sts, k22 to last 2 sts, bind off last 2 sts.
Slip 24 sts from chest onto first st-holder and 22 sts from back onto second st-holder. Sew gap between legs.

Stuffing Stage 1 See page 16.

ARM (make 2)
Hand
With 2 dpns, cast on 3 sts.
Next row: Kfb into each st (6 sts). Slip 2 sts onto each of 3 dpns. Place a marker at beg of rnd. **Rnd 1:** K.
Rnd 2: (Kfb, k2) twice (8 sts).
Rnd 3: K.
Rnd 4: (Kfb, k3) twice (10 sts).
Rnd 5: K.
Rnd 6: (Kfb, k4) twice (12 sts).
Rnd 7: K.
Rnd 8: (Kfb, k5) twice (14 sts).
Rnds 9 and 10: K.
Rnd 11: (Skpo, k5) twice (12 sts).
Rnd 12: K.
Rnd 13: (Skpo, k4) twice (10 sts).

Wrist & Forearm
Rnds 14 to 18: K.
Rnd 19: (K1, m1R, k4) twice (12 sts).
Rnds 20 to 24: K.
Rnd 25: (K1, m1R, k5) twice (14 sts).
Sl last 2 sts from needle 2 onto beg of needle 3.

Rnds 26 to 30: K.
Rnd 31: (K1, m1R, k6) twice (16 sts).
Rnds 32 to 36: K.
Rnd 37: (Skpo, k6) twice (14 sts).
Rnd 38: K.
Rnd 39: (Skpo, k5) twice (12 sts).
Rnds 40 to 43: K.

Upper Arms
Rnd 44: (K1, m1R, k5) twice (14 sts).
Rnds 45 and 46: K.
Rnd 47: (K1, m1R, k6) twice (16 sts).
Rnds 48 to 50: K.
Rnd 51: (K1, m1R, k7) twice (18 sts).
Rnds 52 to 54: K.
Rnd 55: (K1, m1R, k8) twice (20 sts). Rnd 56: K.
Rnd 57: (K1, m1R, k9) twice (22 sts). Rnd 58: K.
Rnd 59: (K1, m1R, k10) twice (24 sts).
Rnd 60: K4, bind off 4 sts, k16 (20 sts).
Beg at gap of bind-off sts, slip 10 sts onto first st-holder and 10 sts onto second st-holder. Bind-off sts form the armpit.

UPPER CHEST
The arms are now joined to the torso. Lay the torso flat with the chest uppermost. Place an arm on each side with the armpit bind-off sts facing towards the torso. Slip sts for arms and torso from st-holders onto 4 dpns as follows (see illus 3):
Needle 1: 10 sts from front of left arm and 12 sts from left chest (22 sts).
Needle 2: rem 12 sts from right chest and 10 sts from front of right arm (22 sts).
Turn doll so back is uppermost.
Needle 3: rem 10 sts from right arm and 11 sts from right back (21 sts).
Needle 4: rem 11 sts from left back and rem 10 sts from left arm (21 sts).
(86 sts in total)
Place a marker for beg of rnd. Rejoin yarn to start of needle 1 (front of left arm) and cont in rnds as follows:
Rnd 1: K.
Rnd 2: K8, k2tog, skpo, k20, k2tog, skpo, k16, k2tog, k22, skpo, k8 (80 sts).
Rnd 3: K.
Rnd 4: (K7, k2tog, skpo, k18, k2tog, skpo, k7) twice (72 sts).
Rnd 5: K.
Leave sts on needles but make sure sts cannot slip off (use point protectors or similar).

Stuffing Stage 2 See page 17 Carefully sew up any gaps between the chest if necessary.

Rnd 6: (K6, k2tog, skpo, k16, k2tog, skpo, k6) twice (64 sts).
Rnd 7: K.
Rnd 8: (K5, k2tog, skpo, k14, k2tog, skpo, k5) twice (56 sts).
Rnd 9: K.
Rnd 10: (K4, k2tog, skpo, k12, k2tog, skpo, k4) twice (48 sts).
Rnd 11: K.
Rnd 12: (K3, k2tog, skpo, k10, k2tog, skpo, k3) twice (40 sts).
Rnd 13: K.
Rnd 14: (K2, k2tog, skpo, k8, k2tog, skpo, k2) twice (32 sts).
Rnd 15: K.
Rnd 16: (K1, k2tog, skpo, k6, k2tog, skpo, k1) twice (24 sts).

Stuff chest firmly. Rnd 17: K.
Rnd 18: (K2tog, skpo, k4, k2tog, skpo) twice (16 sts). Rnd 19: K.

Neck & Head
Rnds 1 to 4: K.
Rnd 5: (K1, kfb) 8 times (24 sts).
Rnd 6: K.
Rnd 7: (K2, kfb) 8 times (32 sts).
Rnd 8: K.
Rnd 9: (K3, kfb) 8 times (40 sts).
Rnd 10: K.
Rnd 11: (K4, kfb) 8 times (48 sts).
Rnds 12 to 14: K.
Rnd 15: K10, kfb, k37 (49 sts).
Rnd 16 (make the nose): K11, (kfb) twice into next st, turn, p4, turn, (k2tog) twice, turn, p2tog, turn, k to end of rnd.
Rnd 17: K11, k2tog, k to end (48 sts).
Rnds 18 to 20: K.
Rnd 21: (K4, k2tog) 8 times (40 sts).
Rnd 22: K.
Rnd 23: (K3, k2tog) 8 times (32 sts)
Rnd 24: K.
Rnd 25: (K2, k2tog) 8 times (24 sts).
Stuff the neck and head firmly.
Rnd 26: (K1, k2tog) 8 times (16 sts).
Rnd 27: K.
Rnd 28: (K2tog) 8 times (8 sts).
Rnd 29: K.
Rnd 30: (K2tog) 4 times (4 sts).
Stuff the head.
Cut yarn leaving a long end, thread through rem sts, pull up tightly and secure yarn end.

FINISHING
See page 16 to add facial features, hair, and other details to personalize your doll (see illus 4).

MATERIALS
- Yarn in the following options:
- 1 x 50g ball Debbie Bliss Rialto 4ply (fingering 100% wool; 50g/196yds) in shade 034 Blush OR shade 038 Mink

OR
- 1 x 50g ball King Cole Merino Blend 4ply (fingering 100% wool; 50g/196yds) in shade 790 Caramel OR shade 929 Fudge
- Small amounts of yarn in preferred color for hair, eyes, and mouth
- Set of 5 x US 3 dpns
- 6 stitch holders
- 8 jumbo pipe cleaners 12" long x ¼" thick

GAUGE
Approx 30 sts and 48 rows = 4" over St-st.

FINISHED MEASUREMENTS
Approx 13" from head to heel.

NOTE: The doll is knitted in rnds from the toes up. The arms and legs are made separately using 4 dpns and then joined into the torso as it is worked on 5 dpns. Stuff the doll and add pipe cleaners where indicated (see p. 16 for stuffing tips).

LEG (make 2)
Foot
With 2 dpns, cast on 3 sts.
Next row: kfb into each st (6 sts).
Slip 2 sts onto each of 3 dpns. Place a marker at beg of rnd. Work in rnds from now on.
Rnd 1: K.
Rnd 2: (Kfb) 3 times, k2, kfb (10 sts).
Rnd 3: K.
Rnd 4: kfb, k2, (Kfb) twice, k4, kfb (14 sts).
Rnd 5: K.
Rnd 6: Kfb, k4, (kfb) twice, k6, kfb (18 sts).
There should now be 8 sts on needle 1 (sole of foot), and 5 sts each on needles 2 and 3 (foot top).
Rnds 7 to 16: K.

Shape Heel
The heel is worked on 8 sts on needle 1 only (work back and forth instead of in rnds).
Row 1: K7, w&t.
Row 2: P6, w&t.
Row 3: K5, w&t.
Row 4: P4, w&t.
Row 5: K3, w&t.
Row 6: P2, w&t.
Row 7: K3, working wrap into st, turn.
Row 8: P4, turn.
Row 9: K5, turn.
Row 10: P6, turn.
Row 11: K7, turn.
Row 12: P8.

Ankle & Calf
Beg working in rnds again:
Rnd 1: K8 from needle 1, pick up yarn strand laying between last st knitted and next st on needle 2, sl onto needle 2 and k tog with next st (this closes gap between heel and foot). K to end.
Rnd 2: Pick up yarn strand laying between last st knitted and first st on needle 1, sl onto needle 1 and k tog with next st (this closes gap between heel and foot). K to end.
Rnds 3 to 6: K.
Rnd 7: K1, skpo, k2, k2tog, k to end (16 sts).
Rnds 8 to 15: K.
Rnd 16: K2, m1R, k2, m1L, k to end (18 sts).
Rnds 17 and 18: K.
Rnd 19: K1, m1R, k6, m1L, k to end (20 sts).
Rnds 20 to 29: K.

Knee
Rnd 1: K1, skpo, k4, k2tog, k to end (18 sts).
Rnds 2 and 3: K.
Rnd 4: K1, skpo, k2, k2tog, k to end (16 sts).
Rnd 5: K1, skpo, k2tog, k3, m1R, k6, m1L, k2 (16 sts).
Rnd 6: K6, m1R, k8, m1L, k2 (18 sts).
Rnd 7: K6, m1R, k10, m1L, k2 (20 sts).
Rnds 8 and 9: K.
Rnd 10: K6, skpo, k8, k2tog, k2 (18 sts).
Rnd 11: K1, m1R, k2, m1L, k3, skpo, k6, k2 tog, k2 (18 sts).
Rnd 12: K8, skpo, k4, k2tog, k2 (16 sts).

Thigh
Rnd 1: K1, m1R, k4, m1L, k to end (18 sts).
Rnd 2: K1, m1R, k6, m1L, k2, m1R, k8, m1L, k1 (22 sts).
Rnds 3 to 5: K.
Rnd 6: K1, m1R, k8, m1L, k2, m1R, k10, m1L, k1 (26 sts).
Rnds 7 to 11: K.
Rnd 12: K1, m1R, k10, m1L, k2, m1R, k12, m1L, k1 (30 sts).
Rnd 13 to 22: K.
Slip 15 sts from needle 1 onto first st-holder (this will be the back of the leg), 15 sts from needles 2 and 3 onto second st-holder (this will be the front of the leg).

TORSO
Join Legs
Use 4 dpns. With RS of facing, slip 15 sts of front of first leg onto needle 1, 15 sts of front of second leg onto needle 2, 15 sts of back of second leg onto needle 3, 15 sts of back of first leg onto needle 4 (60 sts). Place a marker for beg of rnd.

Rnd 1: K14, m1R, k2, m1L, k to end (62 sts).
Rnd 2: K14, m1R, k4, m1L, k18, m1R, k8, m1L, k6, m1R, k8, m1L, k4 (68 sts).
Rnd 3: Skpo, k12, m1R, k6, m1L, k12, k2tog, (skpo) twice, m1R, k10, m1L, k2, k2tog, k2, m1R, k10, m1L, (k2tog) twice (67 sts).
Rnd 4: K13, m1R, k8, m1L, k to end (69 sts).
Rnd 5: Skpo, k12, m1R, k8, m1L, k12, k2tog, skpo, k2, m1R, k10, m1L, k1, k2tog, k2, m1R, k10, m1L, k2, k2tog (70 sts).
Rnd 6: K14, m1R, k8, m1L, k to end (72 sts).
Rnd 7: Skpo, k12, skpo, k6, k2tog, k13, k2tog, skpo, k1, m1R, k12, m1L, k1, k2tog, k1, m1R, k12, m1L, k1, k2tog (69 sts).
Rnd 8: K12, skpo, k6, k2tog, k to end (67 sts).
Rnd 9: K11, skpo, k6, k2tog, k13, m1R, k14, m1L, k2tog, k1, m1R, k14, m1L, k2 (68 sts).
Rnd 10: K10, skpo, k6, k2tog, k to end (66 sts).
Rnd 11: K10, skpo, k4, k2tog, k13, skpo, k12, k2tog, k2, skpo, k12, k2tog, k2 (60 sts).
Rnd 12: K10, skpo, k2, k2tog, k to end (58 sts).
Rnd 13: Kfb, k22, kfb into next 2 sts, k1, skpo, k10, k2tog, k2, skpo, k10, k2tog, k1, kfb (58 sts).
Rnd 14: K

Rnd 15: Kfb, k24, kfb, skpo, k8, k2tog, k2, skpo, k8, k2tog, k3 (56 sts).
Rnd 16: K.
Rnd 17: Kfb, k26, kfb into next 2 sts, k2, skpo, k6, k2tog, k2, skpo, k6, k2tog, k2, kfb (56 sts).
Rnd 18: K. Sl first st from Needle 4 onto end of Needle 3
Rnd 19: Kfb, k28, kfb, k4, skpo, k3, k2tog, k4, skpo, k3, k2tog, k4 (54 sts).
Rnd 20: K.
Rnd 21: K32, kfb, k3, skpo, k1, k2tog, k4, skpo, k1, k2tog, k3, kfb (52 sts)
Rnd 22: K.
Rnd 23: K38, (m1R, k1, m1L, k6) twice (56 sts).
Rnds 24 and 25: K
Rnd 26: K38, (m1R, k3, m1L, k6) twice (60 sts).
Rnd 27: K.
Rnd 28: K38, (m1R, k5, m1L, k6) twice (64 sts).
Rnds 29 to 31: K.
Rnd 32: Bind off 2 sts, k24, bind off 4 sts, k28, bind off last 2 sts (56 sts).
Slip 28 sts from chest onto first st-holder and 28 sts from back onto second st-holder. Sew gap between legs.

Stuffing Stage 1 (see p. 16 for further tips)
Partly stuff foot. Insert pipe cleaners to end of toes. Stuff legs around pipe cleaners. Stuff torso firmly. Distribute stuffing evenly and pad out the shaped sections where appropriate. There is no way of delicately putting this next step . . . pinch the bulge between forefinger and thumb, and with a darning needle sew a couple

of well-placed stitches where your fingers pinch so that it protrudes appropriately.

RIGHT ARM
Hand
With 2 dpns, cast on 3 sts.
Next row: Kfb into each st (6 sts). Slip 2 sts onto each of 3 dpns. Place a marker at beg of rnd.

Rnd 1: K.
Rnd 2: (Kfb, k2) twice (8 sts).
Rnd 3: K.
Rnd 4: (Kfb, k3) twice (10 sts).
Rnd 5: K.
Rnd 6: (Kfb, k4) twice (12 sts).
Rnd 7: K.
Rnd 8: (Kfb, k5) twice (14 sts).
Rnds 9 and 10: K.
Rnd 11: (K2tog, k5) twice (12 sts).
Rnd 12: K.
Rnd 13: (K2 tog, k4) twice (10 sts).

Wrist & Forearm
Rnds 14 to 18: K.
Rnd 19: (Kfb, k4) twice (12 sts).
Rnds 20 to 24: K.
Rnd 25: (Kfb, k5) twice (14 sts).
Rnds 26 to 30: K.
Rnd 31: (Kfb, k6) twice (16 sts).
Rnds 32 to 36: K.
Rnd 37: (K2tog, k6) twice (14 sts).
Rnd 38: K.
Rnd 39: (K2tog, k5) twice (12 sts).
Rnds 40 to 43: K.

Biceps
Rnd 44: (Kfb, k5) twice (14 sts).
Rnds 45 and 46: K.
Rnd 47: (Kfb, k6) twice (16 sts).
Rnd 48: K.
Rnd 49: Kfb, k8, kfb, k6 (18 sts).

Rnd 50: K.
Rnd 51: Kfb, k10, kfb, k6 (20 sts).
Rnd 52: K.
Rnd 53: Kfb, k12, kfb, k6 (22 sts).
Rnd 54: K.
Rnd 55: Kfb, k14, kfb, k6 (24 sts).
Rnd 56: K.**
Rnd 57: Bind off 2 sts, k to last 2 sts, bind off 1 st. Cut yarn, thread through loop. Secure yarn. Beg at gap of bind-off sts, slip 10 sts onto first st-holder and 10 sts onto second st-holder. Bind-off sts form the armpit.

LEFT ARM

Work as for Right Arm to **
Rnd 57: K16, bind off 4 sts, k4 (20 sts).
Beg at gap of bind-off sts, slip 10 sts onto first st-holder and 10 sts onto second st-holder. Bind-off sts form the armpit.

UPPER CHEST

The arms are now joined to the torso. Stuff the arms and insert pipe cleaners after a few rnds of the upper chest have been worked (see p. 16).
Lay the torso flat with the chest uppermost. Place right and left arms on each side with the armpit bind-off sts facing towards the torso.
Slip sts for arms and torso from st-holders onto 4 dpns as follows:
Needle 1: 10 sts from front of left arm and 14 sts from left chest (24 sts).
Needle 2: rem 14 sts from right chest and 10 sts from front of right arm (24 sts).
Turn doll so back is uppermost.
Needle 3: rem 10 sts from right arm and 14 sts from right back (24 sts).
Needle 4: rem 14 sts from left back and rem 10 sts from left arm (24 sts).
(96 sts in total)
Place a marker for beg of rnd. Rejoin yarn to start of needle 1 (front of left arm) and cont in rnds as follows:
Rnd 1: K.
Rnd 2: (K8, k2tog, skpo, k24, k2tog, skpo, k8) twice (88 sts).
Rnd 3: K.
Rnd 4: (K7, k2tog, skpo, k22, k2tog, skpo, k7) twice (80 sts).
Rnd 5: K.
Leave sts on needles but make sure sts cannot slip off (use point protectors or similar).

Stuffing Stage 2

Partly stuff hand. Insert pipe cleaners to end of fingers. Stuff arms around pipe cleaners, evenly distributing to pad out the shaped sections. Distribute stuffing evenly and pad out the shaped sections where appropriate.
Rnd 6: (K6, k2tog, skpo, k20, k2tog, skpo, k6) twice (72 sts).
Rnd 7: K.
Rnd 8: (K5, k2tog, skpo, k18, k2tog, skpo, k5) (64 sts).
Rnd 9: K.
Rnd 10: (K4, k2tog, skpo, k16, k2tog, skpo, k4) twice (56 sts).
Rnd 11: K.
Rnd 12: (K3, k2tog, skpo, k14, k2tog, skpo, k3) twice (48 sts).
Rnd 13: K.
Rnd 14: (K2, k2tog, skpo, k12, k2tog, skpo, k2) twice (40 sts).
Rnd 15: K.
Rnd 16: (K1, k2tog, skpo, k10, k2tog, skpo, k1) twice (32 sts).

Rnd 17: K.
Rnd 18: (K2tog, skpo, k8, k2tog, skpo) twice (24 sts).
Rnd 19: K.
Rnd 20: Slip last st from needle 4 onto beg of needle 1, (skpo, k8, k2tog) twice (20 sts).
Rnd 21: K.
Rnd 20: (Skpo, k6, k2tog) twice (16 sts).

Neck & Head

Rnds 1 to 3: K.
Rnd 4: K1, (kfb into each of next 2 sts, k2) 3 times, kfb into each of next 2 sts, k1 (24 sts).
Rnd 5: K.
Rnd 6: K2, (kfb in to each of next 2 sts, k4) 3 times, kfb into each of next 2 sts, k2 (32 sts).
Rnd 7: K.
Rnd 8: K3, (kfb into each of next 2 sts, k6) 3 times, kfb into each of next 2 sts, k3 (40 sts).
Rnd 9: K.
Rnd 10: K4, (kfb into each of next 2 sts, k8) 3 times, kfb into each of next 2 sts, k4 (48 sts).
Rnds 11 to 13: K.
Rnd 14: K11, kfb, k to end (49 sts).
Rnd 15 (make nose): K12, kfb twice into next st, turn, p4, turn, k2tog twice, turn, p2tog, turn, k to end.
Rnd 16: K11, k2tog, k to end (48 sts).
Rnds 17 and 18: K.
Rnd 19: K4, (k2tog, skpo, k8) 3 times, k2tog, skpo, k4 (40 sts).
Rnd 20: K.
Rnd 21: K3, (k2tog, skpo, k6) 3 times k2tog, skpo, k3 (32 sts).
Rnd 22: K.
Rnd 23: K2, (k2tog, skpo, k4) 3 times, k2tog, skpo, k2 (24 sts).
Rnd 24: K.

Stuff the neck and head firmly.
Rnd 25: K1, (k2tog, skpo, k2) 3 times, k2tog, skpo, k1 (16 sts).
Rnd 26: K.
Rnd 27: (K2tog, skpo) 4 times (8 sts).

Rnd 28: K.
Rnd 29: (K2tog) 4 times (4 sts).
Stuff the head.
Cut yarn leaving a long end, thread through rem sts, pull up tightly and secure yarn end.

FINISHING
See p. 16 to add facial features, hair, and other details to personalize your doll.

BASIC TECHNIQUES

There are some very specific techniques used in this book, so here's a guide to some of the more common ones featured throughout.

Doll Pipe Cleaners

Jumbo pipe cleaners are used (12" long x ¼" thick) inside the dolls; two are twisted together and inserted into each knitted limb as you go. These give extra strength and flexibility than the usual smaller ones.

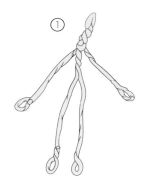

For each limb, twist two pipe cleaners together and curve the end to form a shaped hand or foot (see illus 1). Push to the end of the leg or arm to form the toes or fingers. Once you have stuffed the appropriate section, twist the ends of each leg or arm together to give it some structure, and so there are no loose sharp ends. You will effectively be forming a skeleton as you go! (See illus 1—this is roughly how it will look inside the doll.)

Facial Features

For the eyes, mark lightly with a pencil (or use pins) where you'd like them to go. Using a length of yarn (use cotton for best results) and a sharp needle, work a French knot (see p. 109). Take the yarn to the back of the head and fasten off.

To make the lady's eyelashes, work the French knot and then bring the yarn through to the front again next to the eye and form a very small loop. Take the yarn to the back of the head and fasten off, keeping the loop loose, Cut the loop and trim, fluffing out the ends to form the eyelashes.

The mouth is sewn with red yarn using a backstitch, or cut out some red felt and sew it on with a couple of small securing stitches.

Glasses

Use two standard-size pipe cleaners and wrap them with lightweight/DK yarn in black or color of choice until they are completely covered. Sew in the ends of the yarn. Measure the width of the face, then bend the pipe cleaners to the shape and size of the glasses, personalizing them to your own design. Twist them together to form the bridge and sides.

Hair

The hair is created by knotting lengths of yarn into the head using a crochet hook (similar to rug-making techniques).

1. First decide roughly what sort of style you'd like for your doll—it could be based on someone you know! Have fun choosing the appropriate yarn for the hair—there are some interesting textures out there which make for some fun hairdos.

2. Once you've decided on the hair length, add a bit extra in case of error—it's easier to cut the hair to the desired length and than it is to pull it out because it's too short!

3. Cut a strip of cardboard to the desired length. Wrap the yarn round the cardboard until you have enough to cover the head. Cut the wrapped strands at the bottom and remove the cardboard.

4. Decide where you want your hairline to start, draw it lightly in pencil if necessary as a guide.

5. Insert a small crochet hook through the knitted fabric between stitches. Fold a strand in half and pull it through creating a small loop. Hook the ends through the loop and pull to tighten the knot.

6. Repeat over the head for the desired effect.

Stuffing

The dolls are stuffed as you go along in the following stages:

Stuffing Stage 1

Partly stuff foot. Insert pipe cleaners to end of toes. Stuff legs around pipe cleaners. Stuff torso firmly. Distribute stuffing evenly and pad out the shaped sections where appropriate.

Stuffing Stage 2

Carefully sew up any gaps between the chest where necessary. Partly stuff the hand. Insert pipe cleaners to end of fingers. Stuff arms around pipe cleaners to end of fingers, evenly distributing to pad out. Then stuff more of the torso.

Stuffing Stage 3

When you reach the neck, stuff the rest of the torso.

Stuffing Stage 4

Stuff the head when you only have five rows remaining to knit.

Don't overstuff because this will push the knitted fabric out of shape and the stuffing will show through the knitted stitches. The dolls also need to be positioned, so too much stuffing will lessen their flexibility. The shaped fabric will give you a guide as to which bits need more or less stuffing (calf muscles, thighs, etc). When it comes to stuffing the limbs, make sure each one is even—it's hard to get them identical, but try to get them as similar as possible.

Wrap & Turn (w&t)

Some of the patterns in this book use short rows or partial knitting as a shaping method. The work is turned before the row is completed, and worked over several rows; this creates extra fabric in one area of the knitting. When you turn the work, a hole appears when all the stitches are worked over again. Use the Wrap & Turn technique to hide this hole; in the instructions it is abbreviated to w&t.

Stockinette Stitch

Row 1 (RS): Knit to the turning point. Wrap the next st as follows: slip the st purlwise onto the right-hand needle, bring the yarn forward between the needles to RS of work. Slip the st back onto the left-hand needle, take the yarn back between the needles to WS of work, then turn the work so that the WS is facing.

Row 2: Purl the required number of sts. Wrap the next st as follows: slip the st purlwise onto the right-hand needle, take the yarn back between the needles to RS of work. Slip the st back onto the left-hand needle, bring the yarn forward between the needles to the WS of the work, then turn the work so that the RS is facing.

Each wrapped stitch will have a strand of yarn laying across its base. When the short row section is completed and you work across all the stitches again, knit or purl the strand together with the wrapped st.

Seed Stitch (UK Moss Stitch)

Seed stitch is used often throughout these patterns as it makes for a firmer fabric and neat edges, useful in these smaller items. Depending on the number of sts called for in the pattern, seed stitch is worked as follows:

Uneven amount of sts

Row 1: K1, p1; rep to last st, k1.
Rep for desired amount of rows.

Even amount of sts

Row 1: K1, p1; rep to end.
Row 2: P1, *k1, p1; rep from * to last st, k1.
Rep these 2 rows as directed.

Office supplies closet p. 28

Spa hot tub p. 92

Rooftop p. 98

Roll in the hay p. 36

Vegas honeymoon hotel p. 84

Log cabin p. 20

Camping trip p. 70

Picnic on a hillside p. 78

At the movies p. 64

Naughty Knitting Projects

In the boudoir p. 44

At the beach p. 58

Mile-high club p. 52

The Glowing Triangle

LOG CABIN

Aha, the missionary position you think, a nice easy one—but no, look closer and you'll see that there's a little more to this than meets the eye. The Glowing Triangle involves a bit of a twist, you see; the gentleman can afford to relax a little more while the lady has to work harder than usual—the payoff for her is that she regains more of that vital control that is so often lost in the straightforward missionary.

So you've decided to take a break and escape to your cozy log-cabin retreat for the weekend, and after a day of mountain pleasures and winter sports, you start to relax and get out some marshmallows to toast over a roaring open fire. Things are heating up, the bearskin rug underneath you is feeling delightfully soft and luxurious, and you decide to take things a little further. Warmed by the flames and watched only by the stuffed animals on the walls, you slip off your cozy winter coats and slip into something even more comfortable.

What makes this position so different then? You start off as you would with the missionary, with the lady lying down on her back and the gentleman lying over her, nestling close to her body. He places his knees between hers and his arms either side of her head. She then lifts her hips by pushing up with her feet, taking control of the speed and rhythm. If the position starts to become uncomfortable for the lady, she can place something in the small of her back to reduce the strain, such as a pillow . . . or a bearskin rug.

Just watch what you do with those marshmallow sticks.

BEARSKIN RUG

MATERIALS
- 1 x 100g Erika Knight Fur Wool (superchunky 97% British wool/3% nylon; 100g/44yds) in shade 44 Milk Chocolate
- Small amount of fingering/4ply yarn in Red (for inner mouth) and Black (for nose)
- Pair of US 15 needles
- Pair of US 3 needles
- 2 stitch holders
- Pair of ½" plastic safety eyes

GAUGE
8 sts and 11 rows = 4" over St-st.

NOTE: Main piece is worked in St-st on US 15 needles with Fur Wool in one piece; to begin, each leg is worked separately and then joined to continue the body.

BODY & HEAD
Left Leg
Cast on 3 sts. K 1 row.
Next row (WS): Kfb, p1, kfb (5 sts).
Next row: Kfb, k to end (6 sts).
Next row: K2tog, p to end (5 sts).
Next row: Cast on 2 sts, k to last 2 sts, k2tog (6 sts).

Next row: P to last st, kfb (7 sts).
Next row: Cast on 2 sts, k to last 2 sts, k2tog (8 sts).
Next row: P to last st, kfb (9 sts).
Cut yarn, slip sts onto st-holder.

Right Leg
Cast on 3 sts. K 1 row.
Next row (WS): Kfb, p to last st, kfb (5 sts).
Next row: K to last st, kfb (6 sts).
Next row: Cast on 2 sts, p to last 2 sts, p2tog (7 sts).
Next row: K2tog, k to last st, kfb (7 sts).
Next row: Cast on 2 sts, p to end (9 sts).
Next row: K2tog, k to last st, kfb (9 sts).
Next row: P.

Main Body
Next row: K9 (right leg), cast on 5 sts, with RS facing, k across 9 sts of left leg from st-holder (23 sts).
Next row (make tail): P2 tog, p9, (k1, p1, k1, p1) all into next st, turn, k4, turn, p4, turn, k2tog twice, turn, p2tog, p to last 2 sts, k2tog (21 sts).
Next row: K.
Next row: P2tog, p to last 2 sts, p2tog (19 sts). Work 2 rows.
Dec 1 st at each end of next 2 rows (15 sts). Work 6 rows.
Inc 1 st at each end of next 2 rows (19 sts). Work 1 row.
Inc 1 st at each end of next 3 rows (25 sts).

Right Arm
Next row (RS): Kfb, k5 (7 sts).
Slip rem sts onto two st-holders, 11 sts on first, 8 sts on second.

Next row: Bind off 3 sts, p to end (4 sts).
Next row: K2, k2tog (3 sts). Bind off.

Left Arm
Rejoin yarn to 8 sts on second st-holder.
Next row: K2tog, k6 (7 sts).
Next row: P.
Next row: Bind off 3 sts, k4 (4 sts).
Next row: P2, p2tog (3 sts). Bind off.

Neck & Head
With RS facing, rejoin yarn to 11 sts on first st-holder.
Next row: Bind off 2 sts, k9 (9 sts).
Next row: P9.
Next row: K2tog, k to last 2 sts, k2tog (7 sts).
Next row: P.
Next row: K6, w&t.
Next row: P5, w&t.
Next row: K4, w&t.
Next row: P3, w&t.
Next row: K2, w&t.
Next row: P1, w&t.
Next row: K2, working wrap into st, turn.
Next row: P3, turn.
Next row: K4, turn.
Next row: P5, turn.
Next row: K6, turn.
Next row: P7, turn.
Next row: (K1, k2tog) twice, k1 (5 sts).
Work 3 rows.
Next row: K2tog, k1, k2tog (3 sts).
Next row: K3tog. Cut yarn, pull through loop.

Bottom Jaw
Cast on 7 sts. Work 4 rows in St-st.
Next row: K2tog, k3, k2tog (5 sts). P 1 row.
Next row: K2tog, k1, k2tog (3 sts). P 1 row.
Next row: K3tog. Cut yarn, pull through loop.

Ears (make 2)
Cast on 3 sts. Work 3 rows in St-st.
Next row: P3tog. Cut yarn, pull through loop.

Inner Mouth
Using size 3 needles with red yarn, cast on 3 sts.
K1 row.

Next row (WS): Pfb, p1, pfb (5 sts). Work 2 rows in St-st.
Next row: Kfb, k3, kfb (7 sts). Work 3 rows.
Next row: Kfb, k5, kfb (9 sts). Work 4 rows.
Next row (WS): K (makes halfway ridge for mouth). Work 4 rows, starting with a k row.
Next row: K2tog, k5, k2tog (7 sts). Work 3 rows.
Next row: K2tog, k3, k2tog (5 sts). Work 2 rows.
Next row: P2tog, p1, p2tog (3 sts). K 1 row.
Next row: P3tog. Cut yarn, pull through loop.

FINISHING
Pinch nose slightly, creating more of a point, and sew loosely. Embroider a triangular nose with black yarn (see illus on the left). Sew lower jaw to bottom of head in line with upper jaw. Sew on ears. Attach eyes according to manufacturer's instructions. Sew inner mouth to inside of bottom jaw and top of the head.

MOOSE HEAD

MATERIALS
- 1 x 50g ball King Cole Merino Blend 4ply (fingering/4ply 100% wool; 50g/196yds) in each of shades 929 Fudge (A) and 790 Caramel (B)
- 1 x 100g ball DMC Petra 3 (laceweight/2ply 100% cotton; 100g/306yds) in shade 5310 Black (C)
- Set of 4 x US 3 dpns
- Pair of US 3 needles
- Pair of 1/4" plastic safety eyes

- Thin cardboard
- Toy stuffing

NOTE: All pieces are worked in St-st. The moose head is worked in rnds.

HEAD
With dpns and A, cast on 3 sts.
Next row: Kfb into each st (6 sts). Slip 2 sts onto each of 3 dpns. Place a marker at beg of rnd.
Rnd 1: Kfb into each st (12 sts).
Rnd 2: K.
Rnd 3: Kfb into each st (24 sts).
Rnd 4: K.
There should now be 8 sts on needle 1 (chin) and 8 sts on each of needles 2 and 3 (top of nose).
Rnd 5: K1, (m1R, k2) twice, (m1L, k2) twice, m1R, k4, m1R, k6, m1L, k4, m1L, k1 (32 sts).

Rnds 6 and 7: K.
Rnd 8: K4, m1R, k4, m1L, k11, m1R, k6, m1L, k7 (36 sts).
Rnd 9 and every foll alt rnd: K.
Rnd 10: K4, m1R, k6, m1L, k9, k2tog, m1R, k8, m1L, skpo, k5 (38 sts).
Rnd 12: K3, k2tog, m1R, k6, m1L, skpo, k7, k2tog, m1R, k10, m1L, skpo, k4 (38 sts).
Rnd 14: K20, k2tog, m1R, k9, k2tog, m1R, k5 (38 sts).
Rnd 16: K4, skpo, k4, k2tog, k9, k2tog, m1R, k8, m1L, skpo, k5 (36 sts).
Rnd 18: K4, skpo, k2, k2tog, k4, skpo, k4, k2tog, m1R, k6, m1L, skpo, k4, k2tog (32 sts).
Rnd 20: Skpo, k1, skpo, (k2tog) twice, k1, k2tog, skpo, k3, k2tog, m1R, k6, m1L, skpo, k3, k2tog (26 sts).

Rnd 22: K1, skpo, (k2tog) twice, k5, k2tog, m1R, k6, m1L, skpo, k4 (23 sts).

Rnd 24: K2, m1R, k1, m1L, k7, k2tog, m1R, k4, m1L, skpo, k5 (25 sts).

Rnd 26: (K1, m1R) twice, k3, m1L, k1, m1L, k6, k2tog, m1R, k4, m1L, skpo, k5 (29 sts).

Rnd 28: K1, m1R, k2, m1R, k5, (m1L, k2) twice, m1R, k2, m1R, k1, k2tog, (m1R, k2) twice, m1L, k2, m1L, skpo, k1, m1L, k2, m1L, k1 (39 sts).

Rnd 30: K1, m1R, k3, m1R, k7, m1L, k3, m1L, k5, k2tog, (m1R, k4) twice, m1L, k4, m1L, skpo, k4 (45 sts).

Rnd 32: K1, m1R, k4, m1R, k9, (m1L, k4) twice, k2tog, m1R, k4, m1R, k8, m1L, k4, m1L, skpo, k3 (51 sts).

Rnd 34: K25, k2tog, (m1R, k4) 3 times, (m1L, k4) twice, m1L, skpo, k2 (55 sts).

Rnd 36: K1, skpo, (k2, skpo) twice, k1, (k2tog, k2) twice, k2tog, k8, k2tog, k2, k2tog, k6, skpo, k2, skpo, k7 (45 sts).

Rnd 38: K1, skpo, k1, (skpo) twice, k1, (k2tog) twice, k1, k2tog, k7, k2tog, k1, k2tog, k6, skpo, k1, skpo, k6 (35 sts).

Rnd 40: K1, m1R, (k2, m1R) twice, k1, (m1L, k2) twice, m1L, k6, (k2tog) twice, k6, (skpo) twice, k5 (37 sts).

Rnd 42: K1, m1R, (k3, m1R) twice, (k3, m1L) 3 times, k2, m1R, k4, k2tog, k6, skpo, k4, m1L, k1 (43 sts).

Rnd 43: K.

Slip first 4 sts from needle 1 onto needle 3. Slip last 4 sts from needle 1 onto needle 2. There should now be 15 sts on needle 1 (chin) and 14 sts on each of

needles 2 and 3.

Rnd 44: K15, k1, m1R, k2, m1R, k6, k2tog, k6, skpo, k6, m1L, k2, m1L, k1 (45 sts).

Rnd 46: K1, m1R, k3, m1R, k7, m1L, k3, m1L, k2, (m1R, k3) twice, k2tog, k2, k2tog, k4, skpo, k2, skpo, k3, m1L, k3, m1L, k1 (49 sts).

Rnd 48: K1, m1R, k4, m1R, k9, m1L, k4, m1L, k2, m1R, k4, m1R, k7, k2tog, k2, skpo, k7, m1L, k4, m1L, k1 (55 sts).

Rnd 49: K.

Next row: K52, w&t.
Next row: P26, w&t.
Next row: K23, w&t.
Next row: P20, w&t.
Next row: K17, w&t.
Next row: P14, w&t.
Next row: K11, w&t.
Next row: P7, w&t.

Cut yarn, thread through rem sts, leaving it loose for Finishing.

EARS

(make 2 with A, make 2 with B)
With size 3 needles, cast on 6 sts and work 4 rows in St-st.
Next row: Kfb, k4, kfb (8 sts).
Work 3 rows in St-st.
Next row: K2tog, k4, k2tog (6 sts). P 1 row.
Next row: K2tog, k2, k2tog.
Next row: P2tog twice (2 sts).
Next row: K2tog. Cut yarn, pull through loop.

ANTLERS

SIDE 1 (make 2)
With B and size 3 needles, cast on 6 sts. Work 6 rows in St-st.
Row 7 (RS): Kfb, k to end (7 sts).
Row 8: P to last st, pfb (8 sts).
Row 9: Kfb, k to last st, kfb (10 sts).
Row 10: As row 8 (11 sts).

Row 11: K to last st, kfb (12 sts). Work 2 rows in St-st.
Row 14: Pfb, p to end (13 sts).
Row 15: K2tog, k to end (12 sts).
Row 16: Pfb, p to last 2 sts, p2tog (12 sts).
Row 17: K.
Row 18: P to last 2 sts, p2tog (11 sts).
Row 19: Cast on 2 sts, k to last st, kfb (14 sts).
Row 20: As row 8 (15 sts).
Row 21: As row 7 (16 sts).
Row 22: Pfb, p to last st, pfb (18 sts).
Work 2 rows in St-st.
Row 25: As row 11 (19 sts).
Row 26: P.
Row 27: As row 15 (18 sts).
Rep the last 2 rows (17 sts).
Row 30: P.
Row 31: Bind off 3 sts, k to end (14 sts).
Row 32: As row 8 (15 sts).
Row 33: Cast on 2 sts, k to end (17 sts).
Row 34: P2tog, p to end (16 sts). Work 2 rows in St-st.
Row 37: K to last 2 sts, k2tog (15 sts).
Row 38: As row 18 (14 sts).
Row 39: Bind off 4 sts, k to last 2 sts, k2tog (9 sts).
Row 40: As row 8 (10 sts).
Row 41: K.
Row 42: As row 34 (9 sts).
Row 43: K2tog, k5, k2tog (7 sts).
Row 44: P2tog, p3, p2tog.
Row 45: K2tog, k1, k2tog (3 sts).
Row 46: P3tog. Cut yarn, thread through loop and pull tight. Secure end.

SIDE 2 (make 2)
With B and size 3 needles, cast on 6 sts. Work 5 rows in St-st.

Row 6 (WS): Pfb, p to end
(7 sts).
Row 7: K to last st, kfb (8 sts).
Row 8: Pfb, p to last st, pfb
(10 sts).
Row 9: As row 7 (11 sts).
Row 10: P to last st, pfb (12 sts).
Work 2 rows in St-st.
Row 13: Kfb, k to end (13 sts).
Row 14: P2tog, p to end (12 sts).
Row 15: Kfb, k to last 2 sts,
k2tog (12 sts).
Row 16: P.
Row 17: K to last 2 sts, k2tog
(11 sts).
Row 18: Cast on 2 sts, p to last
st, pfb (14 sts).
Row 19: As row 7 (15 sts).
Row 20: As row 6 (16 sts).
Row 21: Kfb, k to last st, kfb
(18 sts). Work 2 rows in St-st.
Row 24: As row 10 (19 sts).
Row 25: K.
Row 26: As row 14 (18 sts).
Rep the last 2 rows (17 sts).
Row 29: K.
Row 30: Bind off 3 sts, p to end
(14 sts).
Row 31: As row 7 (15 sts).
Row 32: Cast on 2 sts, p to end
(17 sts).
Row 33: K2tog, k to end (16 sts).
Work 2 rows in St-st.
Row 36: P to last 2 sts, p2tog
(15 sts).
Row 37: As row 17 (14 sts).
Row 38: Bind off 4 sts, p to last
2 sts, p2tog (9 sts).
Row 39: As row 7 (10 sts).
Row 40: P.
Row 41: As row 33 (9 sts).
Row 42: P2tog, p5, p2tog.
Row 43: K2tog, k3, k2tog.
Row 44: P2tog, p1, p2tog.
Row 45: K3tog. Cut yarn, thread
through loop and pull tight.
Secure end.

PLINTH

With C and size 3 needles, cast
on 1 st.
Row 1 (RS): (K1, p1, k1) into same
st (3 sts).
Row 2: P.
Row 3: Kfb, k to last st, kfb
(5 sts).
Row 4: Pfb, p to last st, pfb
(7 sts).
Rep last 2 rows to 31 sts. Work
in St-st until plinth measures
4" from point, ending with a
WS row.
Next row: K8, turn, slip rem sts
onto a st-holder.
Next row: P2tog, p to end
(7 sts).
Next row: K.
Rep last 2 rows once more
(6 sts).
Next row: P2tog, p to end
(5 sts). Bind off.
With RS facing, rejoin yarn to
rem 23 sts from st-holder.
Next row: Bind off 3 sts, k9
(including last st used in bind-
off), turn, leaving rem sts on
st-holder.
Next row (WS): P2tog, p to last
2 sts, p2tog (7 sts).
Next row: K.
Rep last 2 rows once more
(5 sts).
Next row: P2tog, p1, p2tog
(3 sts). Bind off.
With RS facing, rejoin yarn to
rem 11 sts, bind off 3 sts, k to
end (8sts).
Next row (WS): P to last 2 sts,
p2tog (7 sts).
Next row: K.
Rep last 2 rows once more
(6 sts).
Next row: P to last 2 sts, p2tog
(5 sts). Bind off.

FINISHING

Attach eyes on head following
manufacturer's instructions.
Stuff head, pull yarn end tightly
to close top. Secure end. With
black yarn, embroider mouth
and nostrils (see main illus).
Antlers: Cut two antler shapes
out of cardboard. With WS
together, oversew each pair
of knitted antlers together,
inserting cardboard and lightly
stuffing either side. Leave a gap
at bottom. Sew antlers to head,
spreading bottom edges out
slightly for a firmer base.
Ears: With WS together,
oversew inner and outer ear
together. Pinch bottom of ear
slightly and sew to head.
Plinth: Press knitted plinth
lightly on WS with a warm iron
over a damp cloth. Using it as
a guide, cut plinth shape out of
cardboard approx 1/4" smaller
than the knitting on all edges.
Sew a running st around outer
edge of knitting. Lay it flat with
WS up. Place cardboard shape
centrally onto knitting and pull
running st to gather edges
slightly, drawing them around
the cardboard to the back. On
WS of the cardboard, sew long
zig zag sts through knitting
from side to side to hold the
fabric taut. Position moose head
centrally onto front of plinth and
sew securely.

HIS 'N' HER WINTER COATS

MATERIALS
For both coats:
- 3 x 25g balls Adriafil Angora Carezza (aran 70% angora/20% nylon/10% wool; 25g/90yds) in shade 02 White (A)
- 1 x 50g ball Sirdar Funky Fur (100% polyester; 50g/98yds) in shade 512 White (B)

For one coat:
- 2 x 25g balls of yarn A
- 1 x 50g ball in of yarn B
- Pair of US 6 needles
- Pair of US 8 needles (for her coat)
- Pair of US 9 needles (for his coat)
- Stitch holder
- 4 press studs

GAUGE
18 sts and 22 rows = 4" using US 9 needles and A over St-st. 24 sts and 28 rows = 4" using US 6 needles and B over St-st.

NOTE: Instructions for his coat are written first, with her coat in brackets: his coat [her coat].

BACK OF COAT
With size 9 [8] needles and A, cast on 36 sts. Work in St-st, dec 1 st each end of every foll 5th row to 28 sts. Work even until back measures 4 1/2 [4 1/4]", ending with a WS row.
Armholes
Bind off 2 sts at beg of next 2 rows (24 sts). Work even until armholes measure 3 [2 3/4]", ending with a WS row. Bind off.

LEFT FRONT
With size 9 [8] needles and A, cast on 20 sts. Work in St-st, dec 1 st at beg of 5th and at same edge (side edge) on every foll 5th row to 16 sts. Work even until front measures same as Back to armhole, ending with a WS row.
** Armhole
Bind off 2 sts at beg of next row (14 sts). Work even until front measures same as Back, ending with a WS row. Bind off.

RIGHT FRONT
With size 9 [8] needles and A, cast on 20 sts. Work in St-st, dec 1 st at end of 5th and at same edge (side edge) on every foll 5th row to 16 sts. Work even until front measures same as Back to armhole, ending with a RS row.
Work as for Left Front from **.

SLEEVES
With size 9 [8] needles and A, cast on 24 sts. Work in St-st, inc 1 st at each end of every foll 4th row to 36 sts. Work even until sleeve measures 4 1/2 [4]". Bind off.

CUFFS (make 2)
With size 6 needles and B, cast on 24 [22] sts. Work 4 rows in St-st. Bind off.

COAT BOTTOM
With size 6 needles and B, cast on 70 [64] sts. Work 4 rows in St-st. Bind off.

HOOD
With size 6 needles and B, cast on 40 [36] sts. Work 2 rows in St-st.
Bind off 6 [5] sts at beg of next 2 rows (28 [26] sts).
Next row: K14 [13], turn. Slip rem 14 [13] sts onto st-holder. Inc 1 st at end of every 4th row to 20 [19] sts. Bind off. With RS facing, rejoin yarn to rem 14 [13] sts, k to end. Inc 1 st at beg of every 4th row to 20 [19] sts. Bind off.

FINISHING
Sew shoulders measuring 1 1/2" and 1 1/4". Mark center of sleeve tops and match to shoulder seam. Sew sleeves to main garment. Sew side and sleeve seams. Sew each cuff into a ring and sew to bottom of sleeves. Sew coat bottom around edge of coat, matching center to center back. Sew top seam of hood and sew to coat. Sew 2 press studs evenly to front.

The Erotic V

OFFICE SUPPLIES CLOSET

The clue is in the title to this one—the V is the shape made by the lady, and it's certainly erotic enough. As you can see, it's a position that involves the gentleman standing up, so it might suit a spontaneous, unplanned situation, an illicit covert encounter in a space not normally considered suitable for this kind of activity, such as an office supplies closet, for example. Why not?!

Work has been taking over your life lately and now you're rushing around to meet a deadline; the stress is starting to get to you—if only you could find something to relieve it. Then you meet a familiar face over a hot photocopier. What a coincidence: you both had an urgent copying job to undertake at the same time. You politely offer to wait while the other person goes first and get to chatting about your work travails. Everybody else has gone to lunch and there's a lock on the door—it seems such a dreadful shame to waste the opportunity.

There is a certain amount of acrobatic athleticism and balance required in the Erotic V, particularly for the lady. She should sit down on a table (or whatever surface is available), while the gentleman stands in front of her, bending his legs slightly. If the surface is too high, he might consider using whatever is close at hand to reach the right height (in this case, his briefcase and a packet of photocopying paper are just the ticket). The lady braces herself by positioning her arms around his neck and putting her legs upward onto his shoulders. She leans back . . . and hey, presto!

Just watch out you don't leave any photocopied evidence.

PHOTOCOPIER

MATERIALS

- 1 x 50g ball DMC Natura Just Cotton (fingering/4ply 100% cotton; 50g/169yds) in each of shades N09 Gris Argent (A), N10 Aswan (B), and N03 Sable (C)
- Small amounts of Red and Green fingering/4ply yarn
- Pair of US 3 needles
- Pieces of sturdy cardboard cut to following sizes:
Front & Back: each 5 ½" x 7"
Top & Base: each 5 ½" x 4"
Two Sides: each 4" x 7"
Lid: 5 ¼" x 3 ¾"
Paper Tray: 3 ¾" x 3"

MAIN PART (worked in one piece)
Front
With size 3 needles and A, cast on 38 sts. Work 4 rows in St-st.
** **Row 5 (RS):** K6A, k2B, k30A.
Row 6: P28A, p4B, p6A.
Row 7: K4A, K4B, k30A.
Row 8: P30A, p2B, p6A.
With A, work 4 rows.
With B, work 2 rows. **
Rep from ** to ** once more.
With A, work 2 rows.
With A, work in seed-st until front measures 4 ¼", ending with a WS row.
Next row: K18A, seed-st 12A, k8B.
Next row: P9B, seed-st 11A, p18A.
Next row: K18A, seed-st 10A, k10B.
Next row: P11B, seed-st 9A, p18B.
Next row: K18A, k20B.
Next row: P20B, p18A.
Rep last 2 rows until front measures 6 ¾", ending with a WS row. Cut off B.

Top
With A, k 1 row. Work 5 rows in seed-st.
Next row (RS): Seed-st 4A, k30C, seed-st 4A.
Next row: Seed-st 4A, p30C, seed-st 4A.
Rep last 2 rows until top measures 3", ending with a WS row. Cut off C.
Next row: With A, seed-st 4, k30, seed-st 4.
Work 5 rows in seed-st.

Back
With A, work 6 ½" in St-st, ending with a WS row. Work 4 rows in seed-st.

Base
With A, work 3 ½" in St-st. Bind off.

SIDE 1
With A, cast on 26 sts. Work 4 rows in seed-st. Work in St-st until side measures 6 ½". Bind off.

SIDE 2
With A, cast on 26 sts. Work 4 rows in seed-st. Work in St-st until side measures 4 ½". With B, work in St-st until side measures 6 ½". Bind off.

LID
Inner: With C, cast on 36 sts.
Row 1 (RS): * P1, k5; rep from * to end.
Row 2 and all WS rows: K the knit sts and p the purl sts.
Row 3: * K1, p1, k4; rep from * to end.
Row 5: * K2, p1, k3; rep from * to end.
Row 7: * K3, p1, k2; rep from * to end.
Row 9: * K4, p1, k1; rep from * to end.
Row 11: * K5, p1; rep from * to end.
Row 12: As row 2.
Rep these 12 rows until work measures 3 ½", ending with a WS row. Cut off C.
Outer: With B, k 2 rows.
Row 1 (RS): * K5, p1; rep from * to end.
Row 2 and all WS rows: K the knit sts and p the purl sts.
Row 3: * K4, p1, k1; rep from * to end.

Row 5: * K3, p1, k2; rep from * to end.
Row 7: * K2, p1, k3; rep from * to end.
Row 9: * K1, p1, k4; rep from * to end.
Row 11: * P1, k5; rep from * to end.
Row 12: As row 2.
Rep these 12 rows until outer lid measures 3 ½". Bind off.

PAPER TRAY
With B, cast on 25 sts.
Row 1 (RS): * K3, sl 1 pwise, k1, yrn, pass slipped st over both k1 and yrn; rep from * to end.
Row 2: P.

Rep these 2 rows until work measures 3", ending with a WS row. Work in St-st until tray measures 3 ¼". Bind off.

FINISHING
Carboard inner: Tape Base, Front, Top and Back together to form a ring, then tape Sides onto this to form a box. Press fabric piece lightly on WS using a warm iron over a damp cloth. Join cast-on and bound-off edge of main part to make a ring. Insert inner. Fit sides around inner, matching correct areas to the frame. Sew sides to main part, matching area in B on front of machine. Join Lid sides with WS facing, insert cardboard and sew up open end. With B, attach lid to main machine with sewn hinges. Repeat same procedure for paper tray and sew it to main machine, placing it at bottom of area in B (see main illus). For each paper tray support, twist together four strands of B to make a 2" long cord. Use to hold paper tray to main machine at a slight angle. Swiss darn buttons (see p. 109) in top right corner of front using C, red and green. Work a handle in top left corner of front.

BRIEFCASE

MATERIALS
• 1 x 50g ball Adriafil Azzurra (fingering/4ply 70% wool/ 30% acrylic; 50g/246yds) in shade 001 Black
• Pair of US 3 needles
• 2 x US 3 dpns
• Several pieces of sturdy cardboard cut to 3 ½" x 2 ½" (enough to make a block ¾" in depth)

TENSION
29 sts & 40 rows = 4".

BACK & FRONT (both alike)
With US 3 needles cast on 24 sts.
Row 1 (RS): * K5, p1; rep from * to end.
Row 2 and all WS rows: K the knit sts and p the purl sts.
Row 3: * K4, p1, k1; rep from * to end.
Row 5: * K3, p1, k2; rep from * to end.
Row 7: * K2, p1, k3; rep from * to end.
Row 9: * K1, p1, k4; rep from * to end.
Row 11: * P1, k5; rep from * to end.
Row 12: As row 2.
Rep these 12 rows until work measures 2 ½". Bind off.

SIDES
Cast on 5 sts. Work 10 ½" in seed-st (when slightly stretched should fit around Front). Bind off.

HANDLE
With 2 dpns, cast on 3 sts. Make 1" length of I-cord (see p. 109). Bind off.

FINISHING
Press pieces lightly on WS using a warm iron over a damp cloth. Tape the cardboard pieces together to form an inner measuring ¾" in depth. Join the cast-on and bound-off edge of the sides to make a continuous ring. Fit the sides around the cardboard inner. Sew the top and base to the sides using a neat, even blanket stitch. Handle: With 3mm dpns, cast on 3 sts and create a length of i-cord measuring 1 ¼". Sew onto the top of the briefcase (see illus).

BLOUSE

MATERIALS
- 1 x 50g ball King Cole Merino Blend 4ply (fingering 100% wool; 50g/196yds) in shade 927 Pale Lavender
- Pair of US 3 needles
- Stitch holder

GAUGE
29 sts and 40 rows = 4" over St-st.

BACK
Cast on 26 sts. Work 3 rows in St-st. K 1 row (hem foldline). Work in St-st, dec 1 st at each end of 3rd and foll 4th row to 22 sts. Work 5 rows. Inc 1 st at each end of next row (24 sts). Work 3 rows.

Armhole
Cast off 2 sts at beg of next 2 rows (20 sts)**. Dec 1 st at each end of next row (18 sts). Work even until armhole measures 1 3/4". Bind off.

FRONT
Work as for Back to ** (20 sts).
Next row (RS): K2tog, k8, slip rem 10 sts onto st-holder.
Dec 1 st at beg of next row and at neck edge on every foll 3rd row until 5 sts rem. Work 2 rows. Bind off.
With RS facing, rejoin yarn to rem 10 sts.
Next row (RS): K to last 2 sts, k2tog.
Dec 1 st at end of next row and at neck edge on every foll 3rd row until 5 sts rem. Work 2 rows. Bind off.

SLEEVES
Cast on 14 sts. Work 4 rows in k1, p1 rib.
Next row: Kfb into each st (28 sts).
Work in St-st, inc 1 st at each end of every foll 8th row to 34 sts. Work even until sleeve measures 3", ending with a WS row.

Top
Bind off 2 sts at beg of next 2 rows. Dec 1 st at each end of next and every foll alt row to 14 sts. Dec 1 st at each end of next 2 rows. Bind off.

TIE COLLAR
Cast on 1 st.
Next row: (K1, p1, k1) into st (3 sts). P 1 row.
Next row: Kfb, k1, kfb (5 sts). Work even in St-st until collar measures 11", ending with a WS row.
Next row: K2tog, k1, k2tog (3 sts). P 1 row.
K3tog, cut yarn, and pull through loop.

FINISHING
Press pieces lightly on WS using a warm iron over a damp cloth. Sew shoulder seams. Sew a running stitch around top of sleeves, pull to gather to fit armholes. Sew sleeves into armholes. sew side and sleeve seams. Fold hem to WS and slip stitch into place. Sew tie collar around neck.

SUIT JACKET

MATERIALS
- 1 x 50g ball Adriafil Azzurra (fingering/4ply 70% wool/ 30% acrylic; 50g/246yds) in each of shades 070 Mélange Anthracite Grey (MC) and 048 Light Mélange Grey (CC)
- Pair of US 3 needles
- 2 small buttons

GAUGE
28 sts and 38 rows = 4" over St-st.

BACK (worked side to side)
With MC, cast on 20 sts.
Row 1 (RS): K to last 4 sts, (p1, k1) twice.
Row 2: K1, p1, k1, p to end.
These 2 rows form seed-st hem. Rep these 2 rows once more.
Row 5: Join in CC, cast on 18 sts, k to last 4 sts, (p1, k1) twice (38 sts).**
Work in St-st stripe patt of 4

rows MC, 1 row CC, working seed-st hem as established, until work measures 4 ½" from cast-on at row 5, ending with a WS row.

Next row: Bind off 18 sts, patt to end (20 sts).
Work 4 rows in St-st. Bind off.

LEFT FRONT

With MC, cast on 20 sts. Work as for Back to ** (38 sts). Work in St-st stripe patt, working seed-st hem as established, until work measures 1 ¼" from cast-on at row 5, ending with a WS row.

Lapel

Next row (RS): P1MC, patt to end.

Next row: Patt to last 2 sts, K1MC, p1MC.

Next row: P1MC, k1MC, p1MC, patt to end.

Next row: Patt to last 4 sts, (k1MC, p1MC) twice.

Cont as established to work 1 st more into seed-st lapel with MC on every row until 10 sts have been worked, ending with a WS row. Cut off CC.

Next row (RS): With MC, work in seed-st to last 2 sts, k2tog (37 sts).

Buttonhole row 1: P2tog, (work 6 sts in seed-st, bind off 2 sts) twice, work in seed-st to end.

Buttonhole row 2: Work in seed-st to last 2 sts, casting on 2 sts over bind-off sts of previous row, k2tog (36 sts).

Next row: P2tog, work in seed-st to end (35 sts).

Next row: Work in seed-st to last 2 sts, k2tog (34 sts). Bind off.

RIGHT FRONT

With MC, cast on 20 sts.

Row 1 (RS): (K1, p1) twice, k to end.

Row 2: P to last 3 sts, k1, p1, k1.

Row 3: As row 1.

Row 4: Cast on 18 sts, p to last 3 sts, k1, p1, k1 (38 sts).

Row 5: With CC, (k1, p1) twice, k to end.

Work in St-st stripe patt, working seed-st hem as established, until work measures 1 ¼" from cast-on at row 5, ending with a WS row.

Lapel

Next row (RS): Patt to last st, p1MC.

Next row: P1MC, k1MC, patt to end.

Cont as established to work 1 st more into seed-st lapel with MC on every row until 10 sts have been worked, ending with a WS row. Cut off CC.

Next row (RS): With MC, k2tog, work in seed-st to end (37 sts).

Next row: Work in seed-st to last 2 sts, p2tog (36 sts).

Rep last 2 rows once more (34 sts). Bind off.

SLEEVES

With MC, cast on 12 sts. Work 2 rows in St-st.

Row 3 (RS): Cast on 6 sts, k to end (18 sts).

Row 4: P.

Row 5: With CC, cast on 6 sts, (k1, p1) twice, k to end (24 sts).

Row 6: With MC, cast on 8 sts, p to last 3 sts, k1, p1, k1 (32 sts).

Row 7: With MC, (K1, p1) twice, k to end.

Row 8: With MC, pfb, p to last 3 sts, k1, p1, k1 (33 sts).

Row 9: With MC, (k1, p1) twice, k to last st, kfb (34 sts).

Row 10: With CC, pfb, p to last 3 sts, k1, p1, k1 (35 sts).

Row 11: With MC, (K1, p1) twice, k to end.

Work in St-st stripe patt, working seed-st cuff as established until cuff edge measures 2 ½", ending with a WS row.

Next row (RS): Patt to last 2 sts, k2tog (34 sts).

Next row: P2tog, patt to end (33 sts).

Next row: Patt to last 2 sts, k2tog (32 sts).

Next row: Cast off 8 sts, patt to end (24 sts).

Next row: Cast off 6 sts, patt to end (18 sts).

Next row: Patt to end.

Next row: Cast off 6 sts, patt to end (12 sts).
Bind off.

COLLAR

With MC, cast on 7 sts, work 4 ¼" in seed-st. Bind off.

POCKET TOP

With MC, cast on 7 sts, work 3 rows in garter-st. Bind off.

FINISHING

Press pieces lightly on WS using a warm iron over a damp cloth. Sew shoulder seams. Mark center of sleeve tops and match to shoulder seam. Sew sleeves to main garment. Join side and sleeve seams. Sew collar to jacket, overlapping lapels slightly. Sew 2 small buttons to front to match buttonholes. Sew pocket top to left front.

SUIT PANTS

MATERIALS
- 1 x 50g ball Adriafil Azzurra (fingering/4ply 70% wool/30% acrylic; 50g/246yds) in each of shades 070 Mélange Anthracite Grey (MC) and 048 Light Mélange Grey (CC)
- Pair of US 3 needles

GAUGE
28 sts and 38 rows = 4" over St-st.

PANTS
Note: Pants are worked from side to side.

FRONT & BACK (both alike)
With MC, cast on 32 sts.
Row 1 (RS): K to last 4 sts, (p1, k1) twice.
Row 2: (K1, p1) twice, p to end. These 2 rows form St-st and seed-st cuff. Rep these 2 rows.
Row 5: With CC, cast on 2 sts, k to last 4 sts, (p1, k1) twice (34 sts).
Row 6: With MC, (K1, p1) twice, p to end.
Row 7: With MC, cast on 16 sts, k to last 4 sts, (p1, k1) twice (50 sts).
With MC, patt 2 rows.
Row 10: With CC, (K1, p1) twice, p to end.
Cont in St-st stripe patt of 4 rows MC, 1 row CC, working seed-st cuff as established until work measures 3 ¾" from cast-on at row 5, ending with a WS row.
Next row: Bind off 16 sts, patt to end (34 sts).
Next row: Patt to end.

Next row: Bind off 2 sts, patt to end (32 sts).
Work 4 rows in St-st. Bind off.

WAISTBAND
With MC, cast on 1 st.
Next row (RS): (K1, p1, k1) into st (3 sts).
Next row: P.
Next row: Kfb, k1, kfb (5 sts).
Next row: P.
Next row: Kfb, k3, kfb (7 sts).
Work even in St-st until band measures 8". Bind off.

FINISHING
Press pieces lightly on WS using a warm iron over a damp cloth. Sew front and back seams, and then inner leg seams. Sew waistband around top of pants, leaving a small overlap at front. Secure overlap.

For shirt pattern see p. 107 and for tie pattern see p. 56.

SKIRT

MATERIALS
- 1 x 100g ball DMC Petra 3 (laceweight/2ply 100% cotton; 100g/306yds) in shade 5310 Black
- Pair of US 3 needles

Work as for Air Hostess Skirt (see p. 54).

The Deck Chair

ROLL IN THE HAY

The Deck Chair: now that sounds nice and relaxing, doesn't it? And to a certain extent you'd be right, although you may have realized by now that most of these positions take a bit of work. Historically this one does come with a backstory—it hit the news a while ago when one of an unfortunate couple experienced back spasms, and they had to be taken to hospital, still in position. Having said that, this is a pretty relaxing one for the lady, so it might be worth taking the risk.

So with that cautionary tale in mind, what's a good setting for the Deck Chair? A nice comfortable spot with plenty of soft padding around. Maybe you've been up since the crack of dawn and have been hard at work tending to the farm—you need a break before you go back to the fields, and what better way to spend it? You collapse in a heap on a haystack and polish off your lunch and wonder what to do next. There's still a little time left before you go back to work . . . how to spend it? Who's there to tell? Well, there's the odd chicken or two pecking around, but they're not going to tell anyone.

For this position, the gentleman sits down first with his legs stretched out in front of him, and leans back, placing his hands behind him with his elbows bent slightly to help him support his weight. The lady faces him and lies back between his legs, using something comfortable to prop her head up (a small straw bale, for example). She then puts her feet onto his shoulders and voilà!

Careful not to spill the milk; there'll be no use crying over it, eh?

CHICKEN

MATERIALS

- 1 x 25g ball Rowan Fine Tweed(fingering/4ply 100%wool: 25g/98yds) in shade 364 Buckden (A)
- Small amounts of fingering/4ply yarn in Yellow (B), Red (C), Black, and Pink
- Set of 4 x US 3 dpns
- Pair of US 3 needles
- Stitch marker
- Toy stuffing
- 2 x pipe cleaners

NOTE: Main part of the chicken is worked in rounds (k every row), starting at the beak and working in rounds towards the tail.

BODY

With 2 dpns and B, cast on 3 sts.

Row 1: Kfb into each st (6 sts). Distribute evenly over 3 dpns (2 sts per needle). Place a marker at end of rnd. K 3 rnds. Cut off B and cast on A.

Rnd 5: Kfb into each st (12 sts).

Rnd 6: K.

Rnd 7: Kfb into each st (24 sts). K 6 rnds.

Rnd 14: K1, * k2tog, k2; rep from * to last 3 sts, k2tog, k1 (18 sts).

Rnd 15: K.

Next row: K10, w&t.

Next row: P8, w&t.

Next row: K6, w&t.

Next row: P4, w&t.

Next row: K6, turn, working wrap into st.

Next row: P8, turn.

Next row: K to end of rnd. K 2 rnds across all sts. Stuff beak and head.

Rnd 18: K1, k2tog, k6, k2tog, k2, (k2tog) twice, k1 (14 sts). Work 2 rnds.

Rnd 21: K1, m1R, k1, k2tog, k2, m1L, k1, k2tog, k to end (14 sts).

Rnd 22: K.

Rnd 23: K1, m1R, k8, m1L, k2, m1R, k2, m1L, k1 (18 sts). K 3 rnds.

Rnd 27: K1, m1R, k3, m1L, k4, m1R, k3, m1L, k2, m1R, k4, m1L, k1 (24 sts).

Rnd 28: K.

Rnd 29: K1, m1R, k5, m1L, k4, m1R, k5, m1L, k2, m1R, k6, m1L, k1 (30 sts).

Rnd 30: K.

Rnd 31: K1, m1R, k7, m1L, k4, m1R, k7, m1L, k2, m1R, k8, m1L, k1 (36 sts). K 5 rnds.

Rnd 37: K1, m1R, k9, m1L, k4, m1R, k9, m1L, k2, m1R, k10, m1L, k1 (42 sts).

Rnd 38: K. Stuff body.

Rnd 39: K40, w&t.

Next row: P10, w&t.

Next row: K8, w&t.

Next row: P6, w&t.

Next row: K8, turn, working wrap into st.

Next row: P10, turn.

Next row: K to end of rnd.

Rnd 40: K.

Rnd 41: K1, skpo, k7, k2tog, k4, skpo, k7, k2tog, k2, skpo, k8, k2tog, k1 (36 sts). K 2 rnds.

Rnd 44: K1, skpo, k5, k2tog, k4, skpo, k5, k2tog, k to end (32 sts).

Rnd 45: K.

Rnd 46: K1, skpo, k3, k2tog, k4, skpo, k3, k2tog, k2, skpo, k6, k2tog, k1 (26 sts).

Rnd 47: K6, k2tog, skpo, k14, w&t.

Next row: P6, w&t.

Next row: K4, w&t.

Next row: P2, w&t.

Next row: K4, turn, working wrap into st.

Next row: P6, turn.

Next row: K8, turn.

Next row: P10, turn.

Next row: K to end of rnd.

Rnd 48: K1, (skpo, k2, k2tog) twice, k2, skpo, k4, k2tog, k1 (18 sts). Stuff body.

Rnd 49: K.

Rnd 50: K1, skpo, k2tog, k to end (16 sts).

Rnd 51: K.

Rnd 52: K2, skpo, k2tog, k3, skpo, k2, k2tog, k1 (12 sts). Stuff tail. K 4 rnds.

Rnd 57: (Skpo, k2, k2tog) twice (8 sts).

Rnd 58: K.

Rnd 59: (K2tog) 4 times (4 sts). Cut yarn, thread through rem sts and pull tight.

WINGS (make 2)

With straight needles and A, cast on 2 sts. Work 2 rows in St-st.

Row 3 (RS): Kfb into each st (4 sts).

Row 4: P.

Row 5: Kfb, k to last st, kfb (6 sts).
Row 6: * K1, sl 1 pwise; rep from * to last 2 sts, k2.
Rep rows 5 and 6 three times more (12 sts).
Row 13: K.
Row 14: K2, *sl 1 pwise, k1; rep from * to end of row.
Row 15: K.
Row 16: * K1, sl 1 pwise; rep from * to last 2 sts, k2.
Rep rows 13 to 16 once more, then rows 13 and 14 again.
Row 23: K2tog, k to end, k2tog (10 sts).

Row 24: As row 14.
Rep rows 23 and 24 twice more (6 sts). Bind off.

COMB
With straight needles and C, cast on 7 sts. Work 4 rows in St-st, inc 1 st at each end of 3rd row (9 sts).
Picot row (RS): K2, yrn twice, k2tog, k1, yrn twice, k2tog, k2.
Next row: P to end, working into double yrn once.
Work 4 rows in St-st, dec 1 st at each end of 3rd row. Bind off.

FINISHING
With black yarn, work a French knot (see p. 109) for each eye. Fold comb in half along picot row with WS facing, sew to top of head. Sew wings to each side of body. Form pipe cleaners into legs, twisting the ends to form claws (see illus). Wrap pipe cleaners tightly with pink yarn. Oversew to body.

HAT

MATERIALS
• 1 x 50g ball Bergère de France Coton Fifty (fingering/4ply 50% cotton/50% acrylic; 50g/153yds) in shade 23132 Cytise
• Pair of US 3 needles
• Set of 4 x US 3 dpns
• Spray starch

BRIM
With 2 dpns, cast on 40 sts. Distribute sts over 3 dpns as follows: 13/13/14. Place a marker at end of rnd.

Rnd 1 (and every other rnd): K.
Rnd 2: * K3, kfb; rep from * to end (50 sts).
Rnd 4: * K4, kfb; rep from *to end (60 sts).
Rnd 6: * K5, kfb; rep from *to end (70 sts).
Rnd 8: * K6, kfb; rep from *to end (80 sts).
Work 2 rnds in seed-st. Bind off.

CROWN
With straight needles, cast on 40 sts. Work 1 ½" in seed-st.
Next row (RS): * (K2tog, k7) twice, k2tog; rep from * once more (34 sts).
Next row: P.
Next row: K2tog, k6, k2tog, k5, (k2tog) twice, k5, k2tog, k6, k2tog (28 sts).
Next row: P.
Next row: * (K2tog, k4) twice, k2tog; rep from * once more (22 sts).
Work 3 rows in St-st.
Bind off.

FINISHING
Spray WS of pieces with starch and press lightly on WS using a warm iron over a damp cloth. Sew crown seam. Sew bound-off edges together to form a trapezoid. Indent top of crown and sew to brim.

DRESS

MATERIALS

- 1 x 50g ball Bergere de France Coton Fifty (fingering/4ply 50% cotton/50% acrylic; 50g/153yds) in each of shades 21365 Nigelle (MC) and 22493 Coco (CC)
- Pair US 3 needles
- Pair US 2 needles
- 2 x stitch holders

GAUGE

30 sts & 48 rows = 4" over St-st with US 3 needles

FRONT & BACK (both alike)

With size 3 needles and CC, cast on 46 sts. Work 2 rows in St-st.
Picot row: K1, * yrn, k2tog; rep from * to last st, k1.
Work 3 rows St-st.
Work gingham pattern as follows.
Row 1 (RS): * K2MC, k2CC; rep from * to last 2 sts, k2MC.
Row 2: P2MC, * p2CC, p2MC; rep from * to end.
Row 3: * K2CC, k2MC; rep from * to last 2 sts, k2CC.
Row 4: P2CC, * p2MC, p2CC; rep from * to end.
Keeping patt as established, dec 1 st at each of every foll 6th row to 28 sts. Work even in patt until work measures 5 ½".
With size 2 needles and MC, work 4 rows in k1, p1 rib.
With size 3 needles, work 12 rows in gingham patt, inc 1 st each end of 5th and 11th row, bringing extra sts into patt (32 sts).
With MC, k 1 row. Work 3 rows in seed-st. Bind off.

STRAPS (make 2)

With size 3 needles and MC, cast on 3 sts. Work 7" in garter-st. Bind off.

FINISHING

Fold hem to WS along picot row and sew in place. Press pieces lightly on WS using a warm iron over a damp cloth and flattening picot hem. Sew side seams. Pin straps to dress top edge (see illus). Sew to top of dress and at point where straps meet top of dress.

TOP

FRONT

With size 3 needles and CC, cast on 22 sts. Work 4 rows in k1, p1 rib. Work 8 rows in St-st, inc 1 st each end of 3rd and 6th row (26 sts).

Shape Armholes

Bind off 2 sts at beg of next 2 rows (22 sts). **
Work even in St-st until armholes measures 1 ¼", ending with a WS row.

Shape Neck

Next row: K8, turn. Cont on these 8 sts only:
Next row: P2tog, p to end (7 sts).
Work 2 rows.**
Next row: Bind off 3 sts, k to end (4 sts).
Next row: P.
Cast off rem 4 sts.
With RS facing, slip 6 sts onto st-holder, rejoin yarn to rem 8 sts, k to end.
Next row: P to last 2 sts, p2tog (7 sts).
Next row: K.
Next row: Bind off 3 sts, p to end (4 sts).
Next row: K.
Cast off rem 4 sts.

BACK

Work as for Front to ** (22 sts). Work even in St-st until back measures same as Front to bind-off sts at shoulder, ending with a WS row. Bind off 3 sts at beg of next 4 rows. Slip rem 10 sts onto st-holder.

SLEEVES

With size 3 needles and CC, cast on 16 sts. Work 3 rows in k1, p1 rib.

Next row (RS): K2, (kfb, k1) 6 times, k2 (22 sts).
Next row: With MC, p to end.
Next row: With MC, kfb, k to last st, kfb (24 sts).
With CC, work 5 rows in St-st, inc 1 st at each end of 3rd and 5th row (28 sts).

Sleeve Cap

Bind off 2 sts at beg of next 2 rows (24 sts). Cont in St-st, dec 1 st at each end of every 4th row to 18 sts. Work 1 row. Bind off.

NECKBAND

Sew right shoulder seam. Using size 2 needles and MC, with RS facing, pick up 6 sts down left side neck, 6 sts from st-holder, 6 sts up right side neck and 10 sts from st-holder. Work 2 rows in k1, p1 rib. With CC, rib 1 row. Bind off in rib.

FINISHING

Press pieces lightly on WS using a warm iron over a damp cloth. Sew left shoulder and neckband seam. Mark center of sleeve bound-off edge, and match to shoulder seam. Sew sleeves to main garment. Sew side and sleeve seams.

DUNGAREES

MATERIALS

- 1 x 50g ball Stylecraft Classique Cotton DK (lightweight 100% cotton; 50g/201yds) in shade 3669 Nocturne
- Pair of US 6 needles
- Stitch holder

GAUGE

22 sts and 28 rows = 4" over St-st.

LEGS
First Leg

Cast on 30 sts. Work 3 rows in garter-st. Cont in St-st, inc 1 st at each end of every 9th row to 36 sts. Work even until leg measures 4 1/2", ending with a WS row.
Cast off 2 sts at beg of next 2 rows (32 sts).
K 1 row.
Dec 1 st at each end of next row (30 sts).
Work even until leg measures 6 1/2", ending with a WS row. Slip sts onto st-holder.

Second Leg

Work as for First Leg, keeping sts on needle after last row.
Next row: K30, then with RS facing, k 30 sts from st-holder. Work 5 rows in garter-st.
Next row: Bind off 22 sts, k16, bind off rem 22 sts.

BIB

With WS facing, rejoin yarn to rem 16 sts.
Row 1: K2, p to last 2 sts, p2.
Row 2: K.

Row 3: As row 1.
Row 4: K2, skpo, k to last 4 sts, k2tog, k2 (14 sts).
Rep rows 3 and 4 twice more (10 sts).
Work 3 rows in garter-st.
Bind off.

STRAPS (make 2)

Cast on 2 sts. Work 6" in garter-st. Bind off.

FINISHING

Press pieces lightly on WS using a warm iron over a damp cloth. Sew front and back seat seams. Sew leg seams. Sew straps to top corners of bib, cross over at back and sew to back waistband 2" apart.

MILK PAIL

MATERIALS

- 1 x 25g ball Anchor Artiste Metallic (super fineweight 80% viscose/20% polyester; 25g/109yds) in shade 324 Dark Silver (A)
- 1 x 50g ball Bergere de France Coton Fifty (fingering/4ply 50% cotton/50% acrylic; 50g/153yds) in shade 22493 Coco (B)
- Set of 4 x US 3 dpns
- 2 ½" x 7 ½" piece of thin cardboard
- Adhesive tape
- Spray starch

NOTE: Milk pail is worked using 2 strands of A held together.

BASE

With 2 dpns and 2 strands of A, cast on 1 st.
Next row (RS): (K1, p1, k1) into st (3 sts).

Next row: P.
Next row: Kfb into each st (6 sts). Distribute sts evenly over 3 dpns (2 sts per dpn). Place a marker at end of rnd. Work in rnds from now on.
Next rnd: P.
Next rnd: Kfb into each st (12 sts).
Next rnd: K.
Next rnd: * Kfb, k1; rep from * to end (18 sts).
Rep last 2 rnds once more (27 sts).
Next rnd: K.
Next rnd: * Kfb, k2; rep from * to end (36 sts) **.
Bind off.

SIDES

With 2 strands of A, cast on 36 sts and distribute evenly over 3 dpns (12 sts per dpn). Place a marker at end of rnd.
Rnds 1 & 3: K.
Rnd 2: P.
K 8 rnds.
Rnd 12: * K8, kfb; rep from * to end (40 sts).
K 7 rnds.
Rnd 20: * K9, kfb; rep from * to end (44 sts).
Rnd 21: K.
Rnd 22: P.
K 5 rnds.
Rnd 28: P.
Bind off.

HANDLE

With 2 dpns and 2 strands of A, cast on 3 sts. Work a 5" length of I-cord (see p. 109). Bind off.

MILK

With 2 dpns and 1 strand of B, cast on 1 st. Work as for Base to ** (36 sts).
Next rnd: K.
Next rnd: * Kfb, k3; rep from * to end (45 sts).
Next rnd: K.
Bind off.

FINISHING

Spray starch onto WS of base and milk and press lightly on WS using a warm iron over a damp cloth, making as flat as possible. Sew base around bottom edge of sides and oversew. Roll cardboard into a cylinder, slightly wider at top than bottom, to fit inside pail. Use adhesive tape to hold shape together and insert into pail. Sew milk into pail, approx ½" below top.

The Eagle

IN THE BOUDOIR

Some pursuits are best enjoyed in the privacy and comfort of your own home, and the Eagle falls in that category. This position can also be enjoyed standing up, but you can't beat the cushioned warmth of your own bed, especially when you've worked so hard to earn a few luxuries in life and your wild days have given way to a more sedate existence.

A nice evening relaxing by the fireside in your nightclothes with a bottle of red wine could ease into an early night. It is a rather nice bedroom after all—you unexpectedly came into some money and used it to settle down into a lifestyle you have become accustomed to. Should you finish reading your book? You glance down at the second volume of *War and Peace* waiting for you on the bedside table . . . maybe there's an alternative? Why not ruffle up the bedclothes a bit, relive your wilder times, and fly like an eagle? After all, Tolstoy will still be there tomorrow night, and although the book is long, life is short.

This position is simple enough to get into and doesn't require any research or spectacular performances. You might even find yourself falling into it naturally without realizing what's happening. The gentleman sits on his knees with his legs bent underneath him. The lady lies on her back facing him and flings her legs wide in the air. He can help her do this by holding her legs gently. He can also raise himself up on his knees slightly if his legs allow him.

A great novelist once said, "A great book should leave you with many experiences, and slightly exhausted at the end"—maybe a copy of the *Kama Sutra* was at his side when he said it.

STRIPED PYJAMAS

MATERIALS
- 1 x 50g ball Bergère de France Coton Fifty (fingering/4ply 50% cotton/50% acrylic; 50g/153yds) in each of shades 21365 Nigelle (MC) and 23132 Cytise (CC)
- Pair of US 3 needles
- 3 small buttons

GAUGE
34 sts and 36 rows = 4" over stripe patt.

TROUSERS
FRONT & BACK (both alike)
With MC, cast on 46 sts. Work 4 rows in garter-st.
Next row (RS): * K2MC, k2CC, k1MC, k2CC, k2MC, k1CC; rep from * to last 6 sts, k2MC, k2CC, k2MC.
Next row: P2MC, p2CC, p2MC, *p1CC, p2MC, p2CC, p1MC, p2CC, p2MC; rep from * to end.
Rep these 2 rows until work measures 4".

Bind off 2 sts at beg of next 2 rows (42 sts). Work 2 ½" even from cast-off sts. With MC, work 4 rows in k1, p1 rib. Bind off.

FINISHING
Press pieces lightly on WS using a warm iron over a damp cloth. Sew front and back seams, then sew inner leg seams. Using a long length of MC and starting at center front, sew a running st around ribbed waistband. Gather slightly to fit waist and tie a bow.

TOP
BACK
With MC, cast on 38 sts. Work 4 rows in garter-st.
Next row (RS): * K2MC, k2CC, k1MC, k2CC, k2MC, k1CC; rep from * to last 8 sts, k2MC, k2CC, k1MC, k2CC, k1MC.
Next row: P1MC, p2CC, p1MC, p2CC, p2MC, * p1CC, p2MC, p2CC, p1MC, p2CC, p2MC; rep from * to end.
Rep these 2 rows until back measures 5". Bind off.

RIGHT FRONT
With MC, cast on 26 sts. Work 4 rows in garter-st.
Next row (RS): K3MC, * k2CC, k1MC, k2CC, k2MC, k1CC, k2MC; rep from * to last 3 sts, k2CC, k1MC.
Next row: P1MC, p2CC, * p2MC, p1CC, p2MC, p2CC, p1MC, p2CC; rep from * to last 3 sts, k3MC.
These 2 rows form garter-st button band and stripe patt.
Rep 2 rows until work measures 3", ending with a WS row.
Next row (RS): K4MC, patt to end.

Next row: Patt to last 4 sts, k4MC.
** Keeping stripe patt correct, work 1 more st into button band on next and every foll alt row until 10 garter-sts have been worked. Work even in garter-st button band and stripe patt until front measures 5". Bind off. Place markers for 3 buttons, the first on the 3rd row and two evenly spaced to beg of collar.

LEFT FRONT
With MC, cast on 26 sts. Work 4 rows in garter-st.
Next row (RS): K1MC, k2CC, * k2MC, k1CC, k2MC, k2CC, k1MC, k2CC; rep from * to last 3 sts, k3MC.
Next row: K3MC, * p2CC, p1MC, p2CC, p2MC, p1CC, p2MC; rep from * to last 3 sts, p2CC, p1MC.
These 2 rows form garter-st buttonhole band and stripe patt. Rep these 2 rows until work measures 3", ending with a WS row, **AT SAME TIME** work a buttonhole on next row and 2 more buttonholes to match markers on Right Front as follows:
Buttonhole row 1 (RS): Patt to last 3 sts, k2, cast off 1.
Buttonhole row 2: K1, yfwd, k1, patt to end.
Next row: Patt to last 4 sts, k4MC.
Next row: K4MC, patt to end.
Work as for Right Front from **.

SLEEVES
With MC, cast on 28 sts. Work 4 rows in garter-st. Work 2 rows in stripe patt as for Back. Bringing extra sts into stripe patt, inc 1 st each end of next and every

foll alt row to 46 sts. Work even until sleeve measures 3 ¾". Bind off.

COLLAR

With MC, cast on 5 sts. Work 3 ½" in garter-st. Bind off.

FINISHING

Press pieces lightly on WS using a warm iron over a damp cloth. Sew shoulder seams. Mark center of sleeve tops and match to shoulder seam. Sew sleeves to main garment. Sew side and sleeve seams. Attach collar to jacket, overlapping with the lapels slightly. Sew on three small buttons to match buttonholes.

BEDSPREAD

MATERIALS

- 2 x 50g balls Rowan Pure Wool DK (lightweight 100% wool; 50g/142yds) in shade 013 Enamel
- Pair of US 6 needles
- 1 x US G/6 crochet hook (for optional shell edging)

GAUGE

22 sts and 32 rows = 4" over lace patt.

Cast on 84 sts. Work 4 rows in garter-st.
Cont in lace patt as follows:
Row 1 (WS): K4, p to last 4 sts, k4.
Row 2: K6, * yf, k2, skpo, k2tog, k2, yf, k1; rep from * to last 6 sts, k6.
Row 3: As row 1.
Row 4: K5, * yf, k2, skpo, k2tog, k2, yf, k1; rep from * to last 7 sts, k7.
Cont in patt until work measures 14 ½". Work 4 rows garter-st. Bind off.

FINISHING

Press pieces lightly on WS using a warm iron over a damp cloth.
Optional Shell Edging: Starting at one corner, using the crochet hook, join the yarn to the bedspread. * Make 5 double treble into one edge st, miss a few edge sts and make a sl st into the edge, miss a few edge sts; rep from * to end, working evenly as you go.

PEIGNOIR

MATERIALS

- 1 x 25g ball Debbie Bliss Angel (laceweight 76% Mohair/24%Silk; 25g/218yds) in shade 033 Soft Grey
- Pair of US 6 needles
- 20" length of ⁵/₃₂" wide ribbon
- 1 small button
- Stitch holder

GAUGE

- 23 sts and 29 rows = 4" over St-st.

SKIRT

Cast on 100 sts. Work 6" in St-st. Bind off.

BODICE (knitted in one piece).

Cast on 36 sts. Work ½" in St-st, ending with a WS row.

Next row (RS): K9, turn. Place rem 27 sts onto st-holder.

Next row: Bind off 2 sts, p to end (7 sts).

Cont in St-st on these 7 sts only for Right Front, inc 1 st at outer edge on next and every foll alt row to 12 sts. Work even in St-st until work measures 2 ½", ending with a RS row.

Next row: Bind off 7 sts, p to end (5 sts).

Work 1 ³/₄" in St-st for back collar. Bind off.

With RS facing, rejoin yarn to rem 27 sts on st-holder, k18 and turn. Leave rem 9 sts on st-holder. Cont in St-st on these 18 sts only for Back until work measures 2 ½". Bind off. With RS facing, rejoin yarn to rem 9 sts, bind off 2 sts, k to end (7 sts). Cont in St-st, inc 1 st at outer edge on every foll alt row to 12 sts. Work even in St-st until work measures 2 ½", ending with a WS row.

Next row: Bind off 7 sts, k to end (5 sts).

Work 1 ³/₄" in St-st for back collar. Bind off.

WAISTBAND

Cast on 7 sts. Work 6 ³/₄" in St-st. Bind off.

SLEEVES

Cast on 26 sts. Work 4" in St-st. Bind off.

FINISHING

Sew shoulder seams. Sew cast-off edges of back collar together and sew to back. Mark center of sleeve tops and match to shoulder seams. Sew sleeves to main garment. Sew sleeve seams. Sew a running stitch along top of skirt and pull up to 6 ½", making even gathers. Sew waistband to skirt, leaving a small overlap. Sew bodice to waistband. Using ribbon and starting at centre front, sew a running stitch around each sleeve cuff (approx 1 ½" from cast on edge). Tie into a bow. Sew button onto waistband opposite the overlapping edge, pushing it through the loose fabric to fasten.

SMOKING JACKET

MATERIALS

- 1 x 50g ball Crystal Palace Cotton Chenille (aran 100% Cotton; 50g/98yds) in each of shades 3501 Mars Red (MC) and 9598 Black (CC)
- Small amount of White fingering/4ply yarn for Kerchief
- Pair of US 3 needles
- Pair of US 7 needles
- 2 x US 7 dpns
- Pair of US 8 needles

GAUGE

16 sts and 18 rows = 4" over St-st.

BACK

With CC and size 7 straight needles, cast on 26 sts. With MC, work 6" in St-st. Bind off.

RIGHT FRONT

With CC and size 7 straight needles, cast on 15 sts.
Row 1 (RS): K1CC, k14MC.
Row 2: P14 MC, p1CC.
Rep these 2 rows for 3 ½", ending with a WS row.
Next row: K2CC, k13MC.
Next row: P13MC, p2CC.
Cont in St-st, work 1 more st into front band on next and every foll alt row until 6 sts have been worked with CC.
Work even until front measures 6", ending with a WS row.
Next row: K6CC, bind off 9 sts with MC.
With CC, work 1 ¼" in St-st for collar. Bind off.

LEFT FRONT

With CC and size 7 straight needles, cast on 15 sts.
Row 1 (RS): K14MC, k1CC.
Row 2: P1CC, p14MC.
Rep these 2 rows for 3 ½", ending with a WS row.
Next row: K13MC, k2CC.
Next row: P2CC, p13MC.
Cont in St-st, work 1 more st into front band on next and every foll alt row until 6 sts have been worked with CC.
Work even until front measures 6", ending with a WS row.
Next row: With MC, bind off 9 sts, k6CC.
With CC, work 1 ¼" in St-st for collar. Bind off.

BELT

With CC and 2 size 7 dpn, work 18" of I-cord (see p. 109). Bind off.

SLEEVES

With CC and size 8 needles, cast on 18 sts. Work 1" in garter-st. With MC, cont in St-st, inc 1 st at each end of every foll 4th row to 26 sts. Work even until sleeve measures 5". Bind off.

POCKET TOPS (make 3)

With CC and size 7 straight needles, cast on 6 sts. Bind off.

KERCHIEF

With white yarn and size 3 needles, cast on 1 st.
Row 1: K1, p1, k1 into st (3 sts).
Row 2: P.
Work in St-st, inc 1 st in the same way at each end of next and every foll alt row to 7 sts. Bind off.

FINISHING

Sew shoulder seams. Mark center of sleeve tops and match to the shoulder seam. Sew the sleeves to main garment. Sew side and sleeve seams. Turn back sleeve cuffs. Sew two pocket tops on fronts (see illus). Sew kerchief to upper left front and sew third pocket top over it.

SLIPPERS

MATERIALS

- 1 x 50g ball Debbie Bliss Rialto Lace (laceweight 100% wool; 50g/426yds) in shade 005 Black
- Small amount of white yarn for pom-poms
- Pair of US 3 needles

SOLES (make 4)
Cast on 3 sts.
Row 1 (WS): K1, p1, k1.
Row 2: Kfb, p1, kfb (5 sts).
Row 3: (P1, k1) twice, p1.
Row 4: Kfb, k1, p1, k1, kfb (7 sts).
Row 5: (K1, p1) 3 times, k1.
Rows 6–11: As row 5.
Row 12: K2tog, k1, p1, k1, k2tog (5 sts).
Row 13: As row 3.
Row 14: K2tog, p1, k2tog (3 sts).
Row 15: As row 1.
Bind off.

UPPERS (make 2)
Cast on 5 sts.
Row 1(RS): (K1, p1) twice, k1.
Row 2: As row 1.
Row 3: Kfb, p1, k1, p1, kfb (7 sts).
Row 4: (P1, k1) 3 times, p1.
Row 5: Kfb, (k1, p1) twice, k1, kfb (9 sts).
Rows 6–12: (K1, p1) 4 times, k1.
Bind off.

FINISHING

Sew 2 soles together to make a firmer base. Sew upper to sole, making a closed toe. Make 2 small pom-poms (p. 109) with white yarn. Trim to desired size and sew to middle of upper.

The Lustful Leg

MILE-HIGH CLUB

No, wait, it isn't as hard as it looks! Okay, so the Lustful Leg does require a certain amount of flexibility on behalf of the lady, but you don't have to be a world-class gymnast, so don't let that put you off—the rewards are certainly worth it. Here's an added bonus: since you're standing up, you can perform it in the smallest of spaces which raises a number of possibilities, particularly where ease of movement is limited.

We all know what a wonderfully liberating experience air travel can be; passengers often find themselves forgetting what they've left behind or what's waiting for them at the other end and start behaving . . . shall we say . . . differently. This might bring out the adventurous side in you, and business trips can quickly turn to pleasure. A quick word of advice: try not to choose a short-haul flight, as any journey time that takes an hour or under will find you up against the clock. Wait until the drinks trolley has gone past and the air stewards are in the galley. One of you should go first, with the other following shortly afterward, a discreet tap on the door and off you go. Things may get a little steamy, in which case don't forget that there are smoke detectors in the toilets. Also, try to avoid the air stewardess on the way out.

The couple should face each other about a shoulder width apart. The lady should then raise one foot and place it onto a higher surface (a sink or ledge would do here). The gentleman then bends his knees and places his shoulder under her raised leg. She puts her arms around his neck and extends her leg as he straightens up, sliding her calf as far up his shoulder as she comfortably can (comfortable being the key word), while he puts his arms around her lower back.

Ladies and gentleman, please fasten your seat belts.

DRESS

MATERIALS

- 1 x 50g ball Bergère de France Coton Fifty (fingering/4ply 50% cotton/50% acrylic; 50g/153yds) in each of shades 23596 Petrolier (MC) and 22493 Coco (CC)
- Pair of US 3 needles
- Stitch holder

GAUGE

29 sts and 36 rows = 4" over St-st.

BACK

With MC, cast on 48 sts. Work 4 rows in seed-st.
Row 1 (RS): K
Row 2 & all WS rows: P.
Row 3: K3, * yo, ssk, k6; rep from * to last 5 sts, yo, ssk, k3.
Row 5: K1, * k2tog, yo, k1, yo, ssk, k3; rep from * to last 7 sts, k2tog, yo, k1, yo, ssk, k2.
Row 7: As row 3.
Row 9: K.
Row 11: K7, * yo, ssk, k6; rep from * to last st, k1.
Row 13: K5, * k2tog, yo, k1, yo, ssk, k3; rep from * to last 3 sts, k3.
Row 15: As row 11.
Row 16: P.
Rep these 16 rows once more, then rows 1 to 8 again.
Next row (RS): * K2tog; rep from * to end (24 sts).
Next row: P2tog, p to last 2 sts, p2 tog (22 sts).
Work 4 rows in k1, p1 rib.
Work in St-st, inc 1 st at each end of next and every foll alt row to 28 sts. Work 3 rows, ending with a WS row.

Armholes

Bind off 2 sts at beg of next 2 rows (24 sts). Dec 1 st each end of next and foll alt row (20 sts).**

Work even until armhole measures 1 3/4". Bind off.

FRONT

Work as for Back to **. Work even until armhole measures 1" from end of shaping.
Next row (RS): K7, slip rem 13 sts onto st-holder.
Next row: P2tog, p to end (6 sts).
Next row: K4, k2tog (5 sts). Cast off.
With RS facing, rejoin yarn to rem 13 sts, bind off next 6 sts, k to end (7 sts).
Next row (WS): P to last 2 sts, p2tog (6 sts).
Next row: K2tog, k to end (5 sts).
Bind off.

COLLAR

With CC, cast on 35 sts. Work 4 rows in seed-st. Bind off.

FINISHING

Press pieces lightly on WS using a warm iron over a damp cloth. Sew shoulder and side seams. Sew collar around neck, matching pointed ends of collar to center of front neck.

TIE

MATERIALS

- Small amount of Red fingering/4ply yarn (or desired colour)
- Pair of US 3 needles

Cast on 5 sts. Work 13" in garter-st. Bind off.

For full suit pattern see pp. 32–34 and full shirt pattern see p. 107.

The Ape

AT THE BEACH

Who hasn't seen the movie *From Here to Eternity* and wondered what it would be like to create their very own slice of beach paradise? Well, here's a suggestion to help you spice up that trip to the coast. It helps if the gentleman has a good, strong pair of legs but don't worry if he hasn't—this is a great workout to help him achieve those all-important quadriceps for the perfect beach body.

And the beach might just be the perfect place for this particular pose; with the sun beating down and the primal scent of gently tanning bodies, things can get a little hot out there in among the dunes. Choose a little-known beach away from the vacationing hoards and while away the afternoon in your deck chairs, perhaps rising every now and then for a leisurely dip in that perfect sea, or a game of volleyball to keep your fitness up. Then, as the sun starts its kaleidoscopic evening descent into the sea, turn your mind to more sensual pursuits. No one's around except the odd seagull here and there, and they're too busy hunting for food.

To perform the Ape, the gentleman should lie on his back and pull his knees up to his chest. The lady then positions herself in a backward sitting position and props herself up on his feet. Not as easy as it sounds—balance is the key here for her, and that all-important leg strength for him. It can help if she shifts her weight on his legs to make his position more comfortable, and she can also grab his wrists for extra support.

So feel free and go ape, but just be careful of that sand—it can end up in the strangest places.

SWIMSUIT

MATERIALS

- 1 x 50g ball Drops Baby Merino (sportweight 100% Merino wool; 50g/191yds) in each of shades 13 Navy Blue (MC) and 01 White (CC)
- Pair of US 3 needles
- Stitch holder

GAUGE

30 sts and 36 rows = 4" over St-st.

FRONT

With MC, cast on 3 sts. Work 4 rows in St-st.

Cont in St-st, cast on 2 sts at beg of next 4 rows (11 sts).

Cast on 3 sts at beg of next 4 rows (23 sts).

Cast on 4 sts at beg of next 2 rows (31 sts). Work 2 rows even.

Dec 1 st at each end of next 8 rows (15 sts). Work 2 rows even.

Inc 1 st at each end of next 7 rows (29 sts). **

Work 3 rows even.

Bind off 2 sts at beg of next 2 rows (25 sts).

Dec 1 st at each end of next row (23 sts). Work 1 row even.

Next row: K2tog, k8, turn. Sl rem 13 sts onto a st-holder. Cont on these 9 sts only.

*** Dec 1 st at each end of every foll RS row to 5 sts.

Dec 1 st at neck edge on next 2 rows (3 sts).

Work 1" in St-st for strap. Bind off.

With RS facing, rejoin yarn to rem 13 sts, bind off 3 sts, k to last 2 sts, k2tog (9 sts). Complete as for first strap from ***.

BACK

Work as for Front to **, ending with a WS row. With CC, k 1 row. With CC, work 2 rows in k1, p1 rib. Bind off in rib.

Leg Frills (make 2)

With CC and RS facing, pick up and k 48 sts around leg edge. P 1 row.

Next row: * K1, kfb; rep from * to end. Bind off.

Sew crotch seam.

FINISHING

Press pieces lightly on WS using a warm iron over a damp cloth. Sew side seams.

WINDBREAK

MATERIALS

- 1 x 50g ball Stylecraft Classique Cotton DK (lightweight 100% cotton; 50g/201yds) in each of shades 3665 Ivory (A), 3670 Saville (B), 3667 Sky Blue (C), and 3663 Soft Lime (D)
- Pair of US 5 needles
- 4 x 8" lengths of 5/16" dowels/wooden craft sticks
- Spray starch

With A, cast on 75 sts.

Row 1 (RS): K1, * p1, k1; rep from * to end.

This row forms seed-st. Work 5 rows in seed-st. Work 2 rows in St-st.

Next row (RS): (k1, p1) twice, k to last 4 sts, (p1, k1) twice.

Next row: (K1, p1) twice, p to last 4 sts, (p1, k1) twice.

These 2 rows form the main patt. Work in patt as follows:

8 rows in B
8 rows in A
8 rows in C
8 rows in A
8 rows in D

With A, work 2 rows in St-st.

Work 6 rows in seed-st. Bind off.

FINISHING

Press pieces lightly on WS using a warm iron over a damp cloth. Spray with starch and press lightly again for a firmer fabric. Oversew a dowel to WS of windbreak at each end. Oversew rem dowels at even intervals.

SEAGULL

MATERIALS

- 1 x 50g ball Rowan Pure Wool 4ply (fingering 100% wool; 50g/174yds) in each of shades 412 Snow (A), 402 Shale (B), and 404 Black (C)
- Small amount of Yellow fingering/4ply yarn (D)
- Set of 4 x US 3 dpns
- Pair of US 3 needles
- Stitch marker
- Toy stuffing
- 2 pipe cleaners for legs

HEAD, BODY, TAIL

With 2 dpns and D, cast on 3 sts.

Row 1: Kfb into each st (6 sts). Divide sts onto three needles. Place a marker at beg of rnd. K 5 rnds. Change to A.

Next rnd: Kfb into each st (12 sts). K 2 rnds.

Next rnd: Kfb into each st (24 sts). K 3 rnds.

Next rnd: K5, k2tog, k2, k2tog, k6, k2tog, k2, k2tog, k1 (20 sts).

Next row: K12.

Return to working in rnds. Work 3 rnds. Stuff the head.

Next rnd: K4, k2tog, k2, k2tog, k5, (k2tog) twice, k1 (16 sts).

Next rnd: K3, k2tog, k2, k2tog, k to end (14 sts).

Next rnd: Kfb, k1, k2tog, k2, k2tog, k1, kfb, k4 (14 sts). Rep last rnd (14 sts). K 1 rnd.

Next rnd: Kfb, k1, k2tog, k2, k2tog, k1, kfb, k1, (kfb) twice, k1 (16 sts). K 1 rnd.

Next rnd: K11, kfb 4 times, k1 (20 sts). K 1 rnd.

Next rnd: K1, kfb, k6, kfb, k1, (kfb) twice, k4, (kfb) twice, k2 (26 sts). K 3 rnds.

Next rnd: Kfb, k3, kfb, k2, kfb, k3, kfb, k1, kfb, k10, kfb, k1 (32 sts). K 2 rnds.

Next rnd: K2tog, k4, kfb, k2, kfb, k4, k2tog, k to end (32 sts).

Next rnd: Rep last rnd (32 sts). K 1 rnd.

Next rnd: K2tog, k4, kfb, k2, kfb, k4, k2tog, k14, w&t.

Next row: P12, w&t.

Next row: K10, w&t.

Next row: P8, w&t.

Next row: K6, w&t.

Next row: P4, w&t.

Next row: K to end of rnd, working wraps into sts. Return to working in rnds. K 1 rnd.

Next rnd: (Kfb, k4) 4 times, k5, kfb, k4, kfb, k1 (38 sts). K 5 rnds.

Next rnd: K1, k2tog, k3, k2tog, k4, k2tog, k3, k2tog, k2, (k2tog, k3) 3 times, k2tog (30 sts). K 1 rnd.

Next rnd: (K1, k2tog) twice, k4, k2tog, (k1, k2tog) 4 times, k2, k2tog, k2 (22 sts). K 1 rnd.

Next rnd: K1, (k2tog) twice, (k2, k2tog, k2tog) twice, k1, k2tog, k2 (15 sts). Stuff the body. Change to C. K 5 rnds.

Next rnd: K8, k2tog, k3, k2tog (13 sts). K 1 rnd.

Next rnd: K2tog, k4, (k2tog) twice, k1, k2tog (9 sts). K 1 rnd.

Next rnd: K2tog, k2, k2tog, k3 (7 sts). Stuff the tail.

Next rnd: K2tog, k1, k2tog, k2.

Next rnd: K2tog, k1, k2tog.

Cut yarn, thread through rem 3 sts and pull tight.

WINGS (make 2)

With B and size 3 needles, cast on 1 st.

Next row: Kfb (2 sts). P 1 row.

Next row: Kfb into each st (4 sts). P 1 row.

Next row: K1, m1R, k to last st, m1L, k1 (6 sts). Work 3 rows in St-st.

Next row: K1, m1R, k to last st, m1L, k1 (8 sts). Work 5 rows in St-st.

Next row: K1, m1R, k to last st m1L (10 sts). Work 11 rows in St-st.

Next row: K1, skpo, k to last 3 sts, k2tog, k1 (8 sts). P 1 row.

Next row: K1, skpo, k to last 3 sts, k2tog, k1 (6 sts). P 1 row.

Next row: K1, skpo, k2tog, k1 (4 sts). Bind off.

FINISHING

With C, sew a French knot (see p. 109) for each eye. Sew wings to each side of body. Form the pipe cleaners into legs, twisting the ends to form claws (see illus). Wrap the pipe cleaners tightly with yellow yarn, forming a webbed effect across the claws.

SWIMMING TRUNKS

MATERIALS

- 1 x 50g ball Drops Baby Merino (sportweight 100% Merino wool; 50g/191yds) in each of shades 13 Navy Blue (MC) and 01 White (CC)
- Pair of US 3 needles

GAUGE

30 sts and 36 rows = 4" over St-st.

FRONT & BACK (both alike)

With MC, cast on 4 sts. Work 4 rows in St-st.

Row 5: K1, kfb twice, k1 (6 sts).
Row 6 & every foll alt row: P.
Row 7: K1, kfb 4 times, k1 (10 sts).
Row 9: K1, kfb twice, k4, kfb twice, k1 (14 sts).
Row 11: K1, kfb 4 times, k4, kfb 4 times, k1 (22 sts).
Row 13: K1, kfb 4 times, k12, kfb 4 times, k1 (30 sts).
Row 15: K1, kfb 4 times, k20, kfb 4 times, k1 (38 sts).
Row 17: K1, kfb 3 times, k30, kfb 3 times, k1 (44 sts).
Cont in St-st, dec 1 st at each end of every foll alt row to 36 sts, ending with a WS row.
Work 4 rows in k1, p1 rib. Bind off in rib.

BELT

With CC, cast on 3 sts.
Row 1: K1, p1, k1.
Rep this row (forms seed st) until belt measures 8". Bind off.

FINISHING

Sew sides. Sew crotch seam. With MC, sew 4 belt loops at the waistband (2 at front, 2 at back). Thread belt through loops and sew ends together.

BEACH BALL

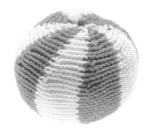

MATERIALS

- 1 x 50g ball Stylecraft Classique Cotton DK (lightweight 100% cotton; 50g/201yds) in each of shades 3660 White (MC) and 3670 Seville (CC)
- Pair of US 5 needles
- Toy stuffing

With MC, cast on 19 sts, leaving a long end for sewing up. K 1 row. Change to CC.
Row 2 (WS): P.
Row 3: K13, w&t.
Row 4: P6, w&t.
Row 5: K8, w&t.
Row 6: P10, w&t.
Row 7: K12, w&t.
Row 8: P14, w&t.
Row 9: K16.
Rows 10–11: Work 2 rows in St-st.
Change to MC. Rep rows 2 to 11 six times more, changing color after Row 11 to create alternating color segments. For the final (8th) segment, rep rows 2 to 10, then bind off, leaving a long end for sewing up.

MAKE UP

With cast-on end, sew a running st along base of ball. Pull tight to gather, secure yarn. Sew cast-on and bound-off edges together. Stuff the ball. With bound-off end, sew a running st along top of ball. Pull tight to gather, secure yarn.

The Perch

AT THE MOVIES

The Perch is a seated position, which means that it might prove suitable in a variety of locations and settings. It gets its name from the way the lady perches on the gentleman's lap and bounces, either delicately or vigorously depending on energy levels and circumstances. Both he and she are facing forward, which makes a multientertainment situation a distinct possibility.

Since this is a discreet position best achieved sitting down, why not mix a bit of culture in with your pleasure and plan a visit to the local movie theater? Unless you feel like giving vent to the exhibitionist in you, try choosing a movie that you think won't attract a wide audience—maybe the local Roxy is putting on a season showcasing an obscure black-and-white avant-garde director who specializes in surreal four-hour features, and oh look, the first showing is at 9:15 a.m. on a Tuesday. It's never too early for popcorn, right? Buy the biggest carton you can get, sit yourselves near the back, and settle down for the artistic marathon to come— make sure no one's behind you or you might get some complaints about blocking their view.

Once the venue has been decided and you've chosen your seats, the gentleman stays seated in his own chair with his legs apart and feet resting on the ground, while the lady sits upright on his lap with her back pressed cozily up against his front. He can hold onto her hips or embrace her around the waist while she performs small "bounce" movements, although she could also lean forward slightly and allow him to control movement.

The bonus is that you both get to watch the movie at the same time, although you might never find out how it ends.

HIS T-SHIRT

MATERIALS

- 1 x 50g ball Bergère de France Coton Fifty (fingering/4ply 50% cotton/50% acrylic; 50g/153yds) in shade 22493 Coco
- Pair of US 3 needles
- Stitch holder

GAUGE

28 sts and 36 rows = 4" over St-st.

BACK

Cast on 30 sts. Work 3 rows in St-st. K 1 row (hem fold line). Work 4 1/2" in St-st from hem fold line. Bind off. Place markers on bound-off edge 8 sts in from each side.

FRONT

Cast on 30 sts. Work 3 rows in St-st. K 1 row (hem fold line). Work 2 1/4" in St-st from hem fold line. Bind off 2 sts at beg of next 2 rows (26 sts). Work even in St-st until armhole measures 1 1/2".

Next row (RS): K10, turn.
Dec 1 st at neck edge on next and foll alt row (8 sts).
Work 2 rows even.
Bind off 4 sts at beg of next row. P 1 row. Bind off.
With RS facing, slip next 6 sts onto st-holder. Rejoin yarn to rem 10 sts, k to end.
Dec 1 st at neck edge on next and foll alt row (8 sts).
K 1 row.
Bind off 4 sts at beg of next row. K 1 row. Bind off.

SLEEVES

Cast on 24 sts. Work 3 rows in St-st. K 1 row (hem fold line). Work 11 rows in St-st, inc 1 st at each end of 5th and 10th row (28 sts).

Sleeve Cap

Bind off 2 sts at beg of next 2 rows. Dec 1 st at each end of next and every foll alt row to 12 sts. Dec 1 st at each end of next row. Bind off 2 sts at beg of next 2 rows. Bind off.

NECKBAND

Sew right shoulder. With RS facing, pick up and k 6 sts down right side of neck, 6 sts from st-holder, 6 sts up side of neck, 10 sts across back neck between markers (28 sts). Work 2 rows in St-st. K 1 row (neckband fold line). Work 3 rows in St-st. Bind off.

FINISHING

Press pieces lightly on WS using a warm iron over a damp cloth. Sew left shoulder and neckband seam. Mark the center of the cast-off edge of the sleeves, and match to the shoulder seam. Sew sleeves into armholes. Sew side and sleeve seams. Turn hems to WS and sew into place.

For shirt pattern see p. 34 and for tie pattern see p. 106.

SKIRT

MATERIALS

- 1 x 50g ball Debbie Bliss Rialto 4ply (fingering 100% merino wool; 50g/196yds) in shade 030 Pink
- Pair of US 3 needles
- Sew-on press stud

GAUGE

28 sts and 36 rows = 4" over St-st.

FRONT & BACK (both alike)
Cast on 48 sts. Work 4 rows garter-st. Work border patt as follows:

Row 1: K2, * yrn, k8, yrn, k1; rep from * to last st, k1.

Row 2: K3, * p8, k3; rep from * to end.

Row 3: K3, * yrn, k8, yrn, k3; rep from * to end.

Row 4: K4, p8, * k5, p8; rep from * to last 4 sts, k4.

Row 5: K4, * yrn, k8, yrn, k5; rep from * to last 12 sts, yrn, k8, yrn, k4.

Row 6: K5, * p8, k7; rep from * to last 13 sts, p8, k5.

Row 7: K5, * k4tog tbl, k4tog, k7; rep from * to last 13 sts, k4tog tbl, k4tog, k5.

Row 8: K.
Cont in St-st, dec 1 st at each end of next and every foll 8th row to 38 sts. Bind off.

WAISTBAND

Cast on 3 sts. Work 8" in seed-st. Bind off.

FINISHING

Press pieces lightly on WS using a warm iron over a damp cloth. Sew side seams together, leaving a 1" gap at top of left side. Sew a running stitch around top of skirt, and gather to 7". Sew waistband around top of skirt, leaving a 1" overhang at side. Sew press stud to ends of waistband.

HER T-SHIRT

MATERIALS

- 1 x 25g ball Orkney Angora Aurora 4ply (fingering 70% angora/30% lambswool; 25g/218yds) in shade 26 Natural
- Pair of US 3 needles

GAUGE

28 sts and 36 rows = 4" over St-st.

Work as for Top from The Deck Chair (see p. 40), using one color throughout.

LEATHER JACKET

MATERIALS

- 1 x 50g ball Regia 4-ply (fingering 75% wool/25% polyamide; 50g/229yds) in shade 2066 Black
- Pair of US 3 needles
- Drinks can ring-pull
- 8 x small rivet studs or small amount of silver metallic yarn

GAUGE

31 sts and 36 rows = 4" over St-st.

BACK

Cast on 35 sts. Work 4 rows in seed-st. Work 14 rows in St-st. Inc 1 st at each end of next row. Work even in St-st until back measures 4". Bind off.

LEFT FRONT

Cast on 23 sts. Work 4 rows in seed-st.
Next row (RS): K to last 2 sts, p1, k1.
Next row: K1, p1, k1, p to end.
Rep last 2 rows once more.
Next row: K to last 2 sts, p1, kfb (24 sts).
Next row: (P1, k1) twice, p to end.
Next row: K to last 3 sts, p1, k1, p1.
Next row: (P1, k1) twice, p to end.
Rep last 2 rows 3 times more.

Next row: Kfb, k to last 3 sts, p1, k1, pfb (26 sts).
Next row: (K1, p1) twice, k1, p to end.
Next row: K to last 4 sts, (p1, k1) twice.
Next row: (K1, p1) twice, k1, p to end.
Rep last 2 rows 3 times more.
Next row: K to last 4 sts, p1, k1, p1, kfb (27 sts).
Next row: (P1, k1) 3 times, p to end.
Next row: K to last 5 sts, (p1, k1) twice, p1.
Rep last 2 rows until work measures 4". Bind off.

RIGHT FRONT

Cast on 23 sts. Work 4 rows in seed-st.
Next row (RS): K1, p1, to end.
Next row: P to last 3 sts, k1, p1, k1.
Rep last 2 rows once more.
Next row: Kfb, p1, k to end (24 sts).
Next row: P to last 4 sts, (k1, p1) twice.
Next row: P1, k1, p1, k to end.
Next row: P to last 4 sts, (k1, p1) twice.
Rep last 2 rows 3 times more.
Next row: Pfb, k1, p1, k to last st, kfb (26 sts).
Next row: P to last 5 sts, (k1, p1) twice, k1.
Next row: (K1, p1) twice, k to end.
Next row: P to last 5 sts, (k1, p1) twice, k1.
Rep last 2 rows 3 times more.
Next row: Kfb, p1, k1, p1, k to end (27 sts).
Next row: P to last 6 sts, (k1, p1) 3 times.
Next row: (P1, k1) twice, p1, k to end.

Rep last 2 rows until work measures 4". Bind off.

SLEEVES

Cast on 21 sts. Work 4 rows in seed-st. Cont in St-st, inc 1 st at each end of next and every foll 4th row to 37 sts. Work even until sleeve measures 4". Bind off.

BELT

Cast on 4 sts. Work 11" in seed-st. Bind off.

COLLAR

Cast on 7 sts. Work 6 ½" in seed-st. Bind off.

SHOULDER STRAPS (make 2)

Cast on 3 sts. Work 1 ½" in seed-st. Bind off.

FINISHING

Press pieces lightly on WS using a warm iron over a damp cloth. Sew shoulder seams. Mark center of sleeve bound-off edges and match to shoulder seam. Sew sleeves to main garment. Sew side and sleeve seams. Sew shoulder straps to shoulders (see illus). Sew collar to back and fronts, slightly overlapping the lapels. Sew 4 belt loops to bottom of jacket (2 at front, 2 at back). Thread one end of belt through hole in ring-pull, fold end over and sew in place on WS. Thread belt through belt loops. Decorate jacket with studs or work French knots (see p. 109) in silver.

The Indrani

CAMPING TRIP

This position is also known as the Indranika or "Queen of Heaven." According to early Vedic and Hindu texts, Indrani was one of the seven Matrikas (mother goddesses) and the beautiful wife of Indra. Indra also just happened to be the leader of the Devas (gods) and lord of heaven . . . a pretty prestigious couple! So you've probably guessed by now that with that kind of history, this is one of the most spiritual positions—you might even feel as if you're staking claim to your own slice of heaven.

So where would be the best place to practice this position? Where you feel closest to the heavens of course . . . in the great outdoors! Choose a nice, clear day, throw on your warm sweaters and hiking boots, and whip up some delicious food to take in your backpack. Then pick a route to go for a leisurely hike to get your energy flowing. As the light starts to fade, find a comfortable spot to pitch your tent—if it's a nice night with a full moon you could always light a campfire and set up your sleeping bag (double, of course) and pillows outside the tent to get a perfect view of the starry skies and wave to Indra and Indrani, happy in their home. Alternatively if the air is a bit too chilly for comfort, snuggle up and get warm and cozy inside your tent.

The Indrani is a position of "high congress," which is a good position for gentlemen of the "well-proportioned" variety. It takes a bit of practice, but due to its relaxed nature it's one of the best for novice *Kama Sutra* devotees. In this position she lies on her back and bends her knees, while he kneels and straddles her hips and thighs as she brings her lower legs over his upper thighs.

Happy camping!

BOOTS

MATERIALS

- Small amount of lightweight/ DK yarn in Brown (MC) and Black (CC)
- Small amount of fingering/4ply yarn in Red (for laces)
- Pair of US 6 needles

SOLE

With CC, cast on 3 sts.
Next row: Kfb, k to last st, kfb (5 sts).
Rep last row once (7 sts). Work 14 rows in garter-st.
Next row: Skpo, k3, k2tog (5 sts).
Rep last row once more (5 sts).
Next row: P3 tog. Cut off yarn and draw through loop.

UPPER

With CC, cast on 27 sts. Change to MC and work 2 rows in St-st.
Next row: K9, skpo, k5, k2tog, k9 (25 sts).
Next row: P9, p2tog, p3, p2tog tbl, p9 (23 sts).
Next row: K9, skpo, k1, k2tog, k9 (21 sts).

Next row: P9, p2tog, p10 (19 sts).
Next row: K6, turn. Working on these 6 sts only, work 3 rows in St-st, ending with a WS row. Bind off. Rejoin yarn to rem 13 sts.
Bind off 7 sts, k to end (6 sts). Work 3 rows in St-st, ending with a WS row. Bind off.

FINISHING

Sew back seam of Upper. Sew the Sole to the Upper. Create laces using the red yarn.

SLEEPING BAG

MATERIALS

- 1 x 50g ball King Cole Merino Blend DK (lightweight 100% wool; 50g/122yds) in shade 018 Turquoise
- Pair of US 6 needles.

GAUGE

22 sts and 28 rows = 4" over diamond patt st.

TOP

Cast on 56 sts. Work 4 rows in garter-st.
Cont in moss-st diamond pattern as follows:
Row 1 (RS): * P1, k7; rep from * to end.
Rows 2 & 8: * K1, p5, k1, p1; rep from * to end.
Rows 3 & 7: K2, * p1, k3; rep from * to last 2 sts, p1, k1.
Rows 4 & 6: P2, * k1, p1, k1, p5; rep from * to last 6 sts, k1, p1, k1, p3.
Row 5: K4, * p1, k7; rep from * to last 4 sts, p1, k3.
Rep these 8 rows until work measures 10", ending with a WS row. Work 4 rows garter-st. Bind off.

BASE

Cast on 56 sts. Work even in St-st until work measures 13". Bind off.

FINISHING

Press pieces lightly on WS using a warm iron over a damp cloth. Pin top onto base, matching lower edges, so base extends above top. Sew around sides and base.

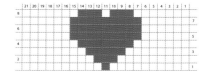

PILLOWS

MATERIALS
- 1 x 50g ball Rowan Pure Wool DK (lightweight 100% wool; 50g/142yds) in each of shades 013 Enamel (MC) and 036 Kiss (CC)
- Pair of US 6 needles
- Toy stuffing

BACK
With MC, cast on 21 sts. Work 20 rows in St-st. Bind off.

FRONT
With MC, cast on 21 sts. Work 6 rows in St-st.
Beg chart: Work 1st row of chart from right to left and 2nd row from left to right. Cont chart to last row.

With MC, work 6 rows in St-st. Bind off.

MAKE UP
Press pieces lightly on WS using a warm iron over a damp cloth. Join back and front, leaving a gap for stuffing. Stuff pillow and oversew gap closed.

TENT

MATERIALS
- 2 x 50g balls Drops Safran Cotton (sportweight 100% Cotton; 50g/174yds) in shade 14 Army Green
- Scraps of contrasting yarn for patches
- Pair of US 5 needles
- Cardboard
- Adhesive tape

GAUGE
24 sts and 32 rows = 4" over St-st.

MEASUREMENTS
12" long x 7 ½" high x 6" wide at base.

MAIN TENT
Cast on 77 sts. Work 6 rows in seed-st.
Next row: Work 4 sts in seed-st, k to last 4 sts, seed-st 4 sts.
Next row: Work 4 sts in seed-st, p to last 4 sts, seed-st 4 sts.
Rep last 2 rows until work measures 16". Work 6 rows in seed-st. Bind off.

BACK FLAP
Cast on 37 sts. Work 6 rows in seed-st. Cont in St-st, dec 1 st at each end of next and every foll 3rd row to 3 sts. Bind off.

LEFT FLAP
Cast on 18 sts. Work 6 rows in seed-st.
Next row: Skpo, k to last 4 sts, work 4 sts in seed-st.
Next row: Work 4 sts in seed-st, p to end.
Next row: K to last 4 sts, seed-st 4 sts.
** Cont to dec 1 st at outer edge on next and every foll 3rd row, maintaining seed-st inner edge, to 1 st. Cut yarn and pull through loop.

RIGHT FLAP
Cast on 18 sts. Work 6 rows in seed-st.
Next row: Work 4 sts in seed-st, k to last 2 sts, k2tog.
Next row: P to last 4 sts, seed-st 4 sts.
Next row: Work 4 sts in seed-st, k to end.
Work as for Left Flap from **.

MAKE UP
Cut 2 pieces of sturdy cardboard 12" x 7 ½". Place together to form tent shape and use adhesive tape to join along top ridge. Mark center of each side of main tent fabric. Sew tent flaps to main tent, matching narrow points to markers.
Patches: Make one or two small squares in St-st with contrasting color and sew to tent using a coarse overstitch or blanket stitch. Fit tent over cardboard frame.

BACKPACK

MATERIALS

- 1 x 100g ball Rico Superba Klassik 4ply (fingering 25% polyamide/75% wool; 100g/459yds) in each of shades 509 Olive (MC) and 104 Brown (CC)
- Pair of US 3 needles

FRONT

With MC, cast on 20 sts. Work 2 ½" in St-st. Work 3 rows in seed-st. Bind off.

BACK

With MC, cast on 20 sts. Work 1 ½" in St-st. Dec 1 st at each end of next and every following 3rd row to 10 sts. P 1 row. Work 10 rows in garter-st. Dec 1 st each end of next and foll alt row (6 sts). Bind off.

GUSSETS (Make 2)

With MC, cast on 6 sts. Work 4 rows in seed-st. Cont in St-st until work measures 1". Inc 1 st each end of next row (8 sts). Cont in St-st until work measures 2". Inc 1 st each end of next row (10 sts). Cont in St-st until gusset measures from halfway along side of Front to center of base (4"). Bind off.

POCKET

With CC, cast on 8 sts. Work 2 rows in garter-st. Inc 1 st at each end of next row (10 sts). Work 14 rows in garter-st. Dec 1 st at each end of next and foll alt row (6 sts). Bind off.

STRAPS (Make 2)

With MC, cast on 35 sts. Bind off.

MAKE UP

Sew cast-on edges of gussets together. Sew gussets around edge of front, matching seam to center of base. Sew gussets to back. Sew pocket to front, fold point down to create a flap and sew down with a few sts. Sew straps to top and bottom of back. Make another small strap for top of backpack in same way as longer straps. Sew in place. Sew a running st through both gussets and Front and draw up until backpack flap closes comfortably. Sew down flap.

FRILLY UNDERWEAR

MATERIALS

- 1 x 50g ball Debbie Bliss Rialto Lace (laceweight 100% Wool; 50g/426yds) in each of shades 009 Cyclamen (MC) and 001 Ecru (CC)
- Pair of US 2 needles
- 2 stitch holders

PANTIES
Front

With MC, cast on 3 sts. Work 4 rows in St-st.
Cont in St-st, inc 1 st each end of next and every foll alt row to 11 sts. P 1 row.
Next row: Cast on 3 sts, k to end (14 sts).
Next row: Cast on 3 sts, p to end (17 sts).
Rep last 2 rows once more (23 sts). Work 3 rows in k1, p1 rib. Bind off in rib.

Back

With MC, cast on 3 sts. Work 4 rows in St-st.
Next row: Cast on 2 sts, k to end (5 sts).
Next row: Cast on 2 sts, p to end (7 sts).
Rep last 2 rows 3 times more (19 sts).
Next row: Inc 1 st each end of row (21 sts).
Work 3 rows in St-st then work 3 rows in k1, p1 rib. Bind off in rib.

Frill

With RS facing, sew Front and Back together at the crotch.

With CC, pick up 15 sts along outside of one leg. Work frill as for Bra. Rep for second leg.

FINISHING
Sew side seams. Using a long length of CC and starting at center front, run a gathering st around ribbed waistband. Secure with a bow at the front and snip off long ends.

BRA
Bra Cup (Make 2)
With MC, cast on 12 sts. Work 2 rows in St-st.
Next Row: K11, w&t.
Next Row: P10, w&t.
Cont to work in short rows until 2sts only have been worked, ending with a WS row.
Next row: K across all sts,

working wrap into st.
Next row: P across all sts, working wrap into st.
Bind off.

Band
With MC, cast on 20 sts. With RS facing, pick up and k 12 sts across lower edge of first Bra Cup. Cast on 2 sts, pick up and k 12 sts across lower edge of second Bra Cup. Cast on 20 sts (66 sts). Work 2 rows in k1, p1 rib. Bind off in rib.

Frill
With CC, pick up and k 24 sts around top of first Bra Cup. Work picot as follows:
Next row: Bind off 2 sts, * slip st from right needle back onto left needle, kfb, bind off these

2 sts just made, bind off 2 sts; rep from * to end. Work a frill around second Bra Cup in the same way.

Straps (make 2)
With MC, cast on 3 sts and make 3" of I-cord (see p. 109). Bind off.

FINISHING
Sew I-cord straps to Bra Cup peaks. Try the bra on the doll and secure the back of the bra band to fit. Using a long length of CC and starting at center front, sew a running st around ribbed band. Secure with a bow at the front and snip off long ends. Darn in yarn ends.

BOXER SHORTS

MATERIALS
- 1 x 50g ball Debbie Bliss Rialto 4-ply (sportweight 100% Wool; 50g/197yds) in each of shades 002 Ecru (MC) and 009 Red (CC)
- Pair of US 3 needles

FRONT & BACK (both alike)
With MC, cast on 35 sts. Work 3 rows in garter-st then purl 1 row. Cont in patt as follows:

Row 1: *K5 MC, k1 CC; rep from * to last 5 sts, k5 MC.
Row 2: P4 MC, * p3 CC, p3 MC; rep from * to last st, p1 MC.
Row 3: As row 1.
Row 4: With MC, p.
Row 5: With MC, cast on 2 sts, k to end (37 sts).
Row 6: With MC, cast on 2 sts, p to end (39 sts).
Row 7: With MC, k.
Row 8: P4 MC, *p1 CC, p5 MC; rep from * to last 5 sts, p1 CC, p4 MC.
Row 9: * K3 MC, k3 CC; rep from * to last 3 sts, k3 MC.
Row 10: As row 8.
Rows 11–14: With MC, work 4 rows in St-st.
Row 15: K7 MC, *k1 CC, k5 MC; rep from * to last 8 sts, k1 CC, k7 MC.

Row 16: P6 MC, *p3 CC, p3 MC; rep from * to last 9 sts, p3 CC, p6 MC.
Row 17: As row 15.
Row 18: With MC, p.
With MC, work 4 rows in k1, p1 rib. Bind off in rib.

FINISHING
Press all pieces lightly on WS using a warm iron over a damp cloth. Sew central seams at Back and Front. Sew inner leg seams. Sew a running st through ribbed waistband and gather slightly to fit waist.

HIS SWEATER

MATERIALS

- 1 x 50g ball King Cole Merino Blend DK (lightweight 100% wool; 50g/122yds) in each of shades 018 Turquoise (MC) and 046 Aran (CC)
- Pair of US 6 needles.
- Stitch holder

GAUGE
30 sts and 32 rows = 4" over patt.

FRONT
With MC, cast on 32 sts. Work 4 rows in k1, p1 rib. Work 2 rows in St-st, ending with a WS row.
Beg chart: Work 1st row of chart from right to left and 2nd row from left to right. Cont to work from chart to last row. Work 4 rows in St-st.

Shape Shoulders & Neck
Next row: K11 sts, turn.
Next row: P2tog, p to end (10 sts).
Next row: K to last 2 sts, k2tog (9 sts). Work 2 rows in St-st. Bind off. Place central 10 sts onto st-holder, k rem 11 sts.
Next row: P to last 2 sts, p2tog (10 sts).
Next row: K2tog, k to end (9 sts). Work 2 rows in St-st. Bind off.

BACK
With MC, cast on 32 sts. Work 4 rows in k1, p1 rib. Work even in St-st until work measures same as Front to bound-off edge at shoulders. Bind off. On the top edge, mark 14 sts of back neck.

SLEEVES
With MC, cast on 18 sts. Work in k1, p1 rib for 4 rows. Cont in St-st, inc 1 st each end of next and every foll 3rd row to 36 sts. Work 3 rows even in St-st, ending with a WS row. Bind off.

COLLAR
Join right shoulder seam. With MC and RS facing, pick up and k 5 sts down left front neck, 10 sts from st-holder, 5 sts up right side of neck, 14 sts from back neck (34 sts). Work 3 rows in k1, p1 rib. Bind off in rib.

FINISHING
Press pieces lightly on WS using a warm iron over a damp cloth. Sew left shoulder seam. Mark center of sleeve tops and match to shoulder seams. Sew sleeves to main garment. Sew side and sleeve seams.

HER SWEATER

MATERIALS

- 1 x 50g ball Drops Baby Merino (sportweight 100% Merino wool; 50g/191yds)in each of shades 13 Navy Blue (MC) and 01 White (CC)
- Pair US 3 needles

GAUGE
30 sts and 36 rows = 4" over St-st.

FRONT & BACK (both alike)
With MC, cast on 40 sts. Work 4 rows in garter-st.
Cont in St-st stripe patt of 2 rows in CC and 2 rows in MC until work measures 2 ½". Cont to work in CC only until work measures 4 ½". With MC, work 4 rows in garter-st. Bind off.

SLEEVES
With MC, cast on 16 sts. Work 4 rows in garter-st.
Cont in St-st stripe patt of 2 rows in CC and 2 rows in MC, at the same time inc 1 st each end of 1st and every foll 5th row to 30 sts ending on a WS row. Bind off.

FINISHING
Press pieces lightly on WS using a warm iron over damp cloth. Mark shoulder seams ¾" from armhole edges and join. Mark center of sleeve tops and match to shoulder seams. Sew side and sleeve seams.

The Kneel

PICNIC ON A HILLSIDE

The Kneel is a cozy, affectionate position, which could start out innocently enough in a warm embrace and lead to something further. You don't need to be agile or to have trained to the peak of physical fitness to enjoy this one. It's a nice, slow way to rediscover your intimacy as you face each other and gaze into each other's eyes.

The Kneel would suit a more relaxed situation—maybe the sun has finally come out after a long winter, and you decide to call in sick and take a spontaneous day off work. You drive to an isolated spot with breathtaking views and drink it all in, clearing the cobwebs. Perhaps the knitting has made it into the car too, needles clacking away on the journey down as the radio sends out your favorite tunes, and you both catch up about life. You find the perfect spot, you unpack the picnic plus your tartan rug and walk to a more isolated area. There's not a person or a thing around for miles, save a solitary lighthouse in the distance. You hug, you kiss, one thing leads to another . . .

Here's how to make this position work—the gentleman kneels down facing the lady, who then sits in his lap with her knees either side of his thighs and her shins on the floor (alternatively she could balance on his calves). She wraps her arms tightly around his neck and he embraces her around the waist or stomach; they then rock gently in the breeze. You can keep this going as long as his legs don't go to sleep (or until you spot some fellow picnickers on the horizon, depending on which occurs first).

One word of warning—you might not get much knitting done.

POLO NECK SWEATER

MATERIALS

- 1 x 50g ball Adriafil Azzurra (fingering/4ply 70% wool/30% acrylic; 50g/246yds) in 001 Black
- Pair of US 3 needles

GAUGE

29 sts and 42 rows = 4" over St-st.

BACK & FRONT (both alike)

Cast on 30 sts. Work 6 rows in k1, p1 rib. Cont in St-st until work measures 5".

Next row (RS): Bind off 7 sts, k16, bind off rem 7 sts.

With RS facing, rejoin yarn to rem 16 sts. Work 1 ½" in k1, p1 rib for roll neck. Bind off in rib.

SLEEVES

Cast on 18 sts. Work 4 rows in k1, p1 rib. Work in St-st, inc 1 st each end of 3rd and every foll 6th row to 32 sts. Work even until sleeve measures 4 ½". Bind off.

FINISHING

Press pieces lightly on WS using a warm iron over a damp cloth. Sew shoulder and roll neck seams. Mark center of sleeve tops and match to shoulder seam. Sew sleeves to main garment. Sew side and sleeve seams.

PICNIC RUG

MATERIALS

- 1 x 50g ball Adriafil Azzurra (70% wool/30% acrylic; 50g/246yds) in each of shades 017 Red (A), 001 Black (B), and 002 White (C)
- 1 pair 3mm needles

NOTE: The blanket is worked according to the chart, with a moss-st border worked over 4 sts in A at either side, and over 6 rows in A at the top and bottom. It's advisable to treat each patt repeat as a self-contained unit and use separate lengths of yarn.

INSTRUCTIONS

With A, cast on 86 sts. Work 6 rows in moss-st.

Row 1: K1A, p1A, k1A, p1A, *work per the chart; rep from * twice more, k1A, p1A, k1A, p1A.

Row 2: P1A, k1A, p1A, k1A, *work per the chart; rep from * twice more, p1A, k1A, p1A, k1A.

Cont in patt following the established moss-st border in A over 4 sts, and continuing to work 3 patt reps over a row. Rep the patt 3 times over the length of the blanket so that the blanket is made up of 9 square repeats overall. Work 6 rows in moss-st in A. Bind off.

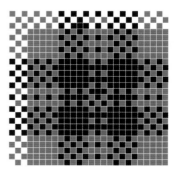

DRESS AND HEADSCARF

MATERIALS

- 1 x 100g ball DMC Petra 3 (laceweight/2ply 100% cotton; 100g/306yds) in each of shades 5145 Pale Blue (MC) and Ecru (CC)
- Pair of US 3 needles

GAUGE

29 sts and 38 rows = 4" over St-st.

DRESS
BACK & FRONT (both alike)

With MC, cast on 38 sts. Work 3 rows in St-st. K 1 row (hem foldline). Work in St-st, dec 1 st each end of every foll 8th row to 30 sts. Work in St-st until work measures 4", ending with a WS row.

Armholes

Bind off 2 sts at beg of next 2 rows (34 sts). Dec 1 st at each end of every foll alt row to 20 sts.

With CC, work in St-st shaping until armholes measure 2". Bind off 3 sts at beg of next 2 rows (14 sts). Work 3 rows in St-st, ending with a RS row. K 1 row (hem foldline). Work 3 rows in St-st. Bind off.

HALF BELT

With CC, cast on 5 sts, work 1 ½" in St-st. Bind off.

BUTTONS

With MC, cast on 1 st.
Row 1 (RS): (K1, p1, k1) into st (3 sts).
Rows 2 & 4: P.
Row 3: Kfb, k1, kfb (5 sts).
Row 5: K.
Row 6: P2tog, p1, p2tog (3 sts).
Row 7: K3tog. Cut yarn, pull through last st and secure.

HEADSCARF

With CC, cast on 1 st.
Row 1 (RS): (K1, p1, k1) into st (3 sts).
Row 2: Kfb, p1, kfb (5 sts).
Row 3: KfbCC, k1CC, p1MC, k1CC, kfbCC (7 sts).
Row 4: KfbCC, p1CC, k1MC, p1MC, k1MC, p1CC, kfbCC (9 sts).
Row 5: KfbCC, k1CC, (p1MC, k1MC) twice, p1MC, k1CC, kfbCC (11 sts).
Work in seed-st and border patt as established, inc 1 st at each end of every row to 65 sts.
With CC, work 4 rows of seed-st, inc 1 st each end of every row (73 sts). Bind off.

FINISHING

Press pieces lightly on WS using a warm iron over a damp cloth. Sew shoulder and side seams. Fold hems to WS and oversew in place. Sew belt to front of dress and sew buttons at each end (see illus).

BASKET

MATERIALS

- 1 x 50g ball 3ply Natural Jute Twine (50g/131yds)
- Small amount of Dark Brown lightweight/DK yarn for toggles and handle
- Pair of US 5 needles
- Set of 4 x US 3 dpns
- Piece of gingham fabric and matching sewing thread (optional)
- Small amount of White fingering/4ply yarn for plate
- Spray starch

BASE & LID (both alike)
Cast on 16 sts. Work 2 ½" in garter-st. Bind off.

SIDES
Cast on 52 sts. Work 1" in garter-st. Bind off.

PLATE
With 1 strand of white yarn and dpns, work as for Milk Pail Base (see p. 42) to 27 sts, then proceed as follows:
Next rnd: P.
Next rnd: (Pfb, p2) 9 times (36 sts).
Next rnd: P.
Bind off.

FINISHING
Sew edges of basket sides together to form a ring. Sew base to sides. Pinch corners of sides slightly and sew to form a sharper edge. Attach lid to basket using brown yarn to sew hinges. With brown yarn, work a 1 ½" length of I-cord (see p. 109) and sew to front of basket as a handle. With brown yarn, sew two large French knots (see p. 109) either side of handle. Sew two loops to edge of lid to match bobbles. To line basket lid with gingham, cut a piece of fabric slightly larger than lid, fold raw edges to WS and press. Using sewing thread, sew gingham to lid. Spray starch onto WS of plate and press lightly on WS using a warm iron over a damp cloth to stiffen. With brown yarn, sew two crossed straps to gingham lining or basket lid to hold the plate (see illus).

KNITTING

MATERIALS
For the knitting:
- 2 cocktail sticks
- 2 small wooden beads ¼" diameter
- Small amount of laceweight/2ply yarn
- Pair of US 0 needles

Knitting project: Cut each cocktail stick to 2" and stick a bead onto cut end to make knitting needles. With size 0 needles and laceweight yarn, work a few rows in a stitch of your choice then slip sts onto cocktail stick needles. Wind rem yarn into a small ball and secure with a few stitches.

The Suspended Scissors

VEGAS HONEYMOON HOTEL

Well now, here's an interesting proposition, and definitely aimed at the more athletic among us. Allegedly it's addictive once you get used to it, but some of us lesser mortals will have to take the aficionados at their word without actually putting it to the test. If you're feeling adventurous enough to try it, make sure the lady has enough strength in her arms to keep herself propped up, otherwise carpet burns are a distinct possibility.

Since this is one of the more risky positions, it might work best if you have some adrenaline pumping through your veins. You've been promising yourself the road trip of a lifetime since you were a teenager so you decide to seize the moment. You stop at a midwestern gas station and meet some kindred spirits, hell-bent on reliving their youth. Next stop? Vegas, baby! After a madcap night which you seem to remember ended up at an Elvis wedding chapel, you hit the casinos, and what do you know? Lady Luck is on your side, and you win big. Still on a high and determined to celebrate, you book yourselves into the most expensive Vegas suite you can find . . . this is a night you won't forget.

To get into position, the lady lies off the edge of the bed on her side (she can also rest her calves, ankles, and feet on the bed itself) and supports herself with her left arm. The gentleman holds her up from the waist, stands astride her left leg, and eases himself toward her, intersecting her legs and making sure that she stays sideways. She can then hold onto his arm for extra support.

What happens in Vegas . . . well, you know the rest of the saying.

HEADBOARD

MATERIALS
- 2 x 50g balls Rowan Pure Wool DK (lightweight 100% wool; 50g/142yds) in shade 036 Kiss (A)
- Pair of US 6 needles
- Stitch holder
- 13" x 10" piece of 1" thick upholstery foam
- Toy stuffing

GAUGE
23 sts and 32 rows = 4" over St-st.

HEADBOARD
Cast on 54 sts.
Row 1 (RS): K1, * k3, p1; rep from * to last st, k1.
Row 2 & all WS rows: P.
Row 3: Kfb, k to last st, kfb (56 sts).
Row 5: K3, * p1, k3; rep from * to last st, k1.
Row 7: Kfb, k to last st, kfb (58 sts).
Row 8: P.
These 8 rows form patt. Rep these 8 rows, inc 1 st at each end of every 3rd row to 78 sts, working extra sts into patt. Work even in patt until headboard measures 8", ending with a WS row.

TOP
Next row (RS): Patt 39 sts, slip rem 39 sts onto a st-holder.
Next row: P.
Next row: K2tog, patt to end (38 sts).
Patt 2 rows.
Next row: Patt to last 2 sts, p2tog (37 sts).
Patt 2 rows.
Next row: K2tog, patt to end (36 sts).
Next row: P2tog, patt to end (35 sts).
Rep last 2 rows to 26 sts. Work in patt, dec 1 st at each end of next 5 rows (16 sts). Bind off.
With RS facing, rejoin yarn to rem 39 sts. Patt 2 rows.
Next row (RS): Patt to last 2 sts, k2tog (38 sts).
Patt 2 rows.
Next row: P2tog, p to end (37 sts).
Patt 2 rows.
Next row: Patt to last 2 sts, k2tog (36 sts).
Next row: Patt to last 2 sts, p2tog (35 sts).
Rep last 2 rows to 26 sts. Work in patt, dec 1 st at each end of next 5 rows (16 sts). Bind off.

FINISHING
Press lightly on WS using a warm iron over a damp cloth. Sew a running st around outer edge of headboard fabric. Cut headboard shape from foam using the knitted fabric as a guide, making sure the foam shape is approx 2" smaller than the fabric all round. Lay knitted fabric with RS down onto an even surface. Spread a thin of layer of toy stuffing evenly over surface to pad headboard. Place foam shape centrally onto stuffed headboard. Draw up running st to gather edges loosely and evenly, pulling edges of fabric around foam to WS. Adjust stuffing in front of headboard, adding more if desired around the sides. Oversew edges of fabric to WS of foam.

Indents: Use pins to mark even points where you'd place them. Thread a sharp needle with a length of yarn and knot the end. Secure yarn to WS of foam at back of headboard. Insert needle from back to front at first marker, make a small stitch and pull through to the back. Pull tight to make an indent. Sew securely and repeat for each marker.

BEDSPREAD

MATERIALS
- 2 x 50g balls King Cole Moments (lightweight/DK 100% polyester; 50g/98yds) in shade 477 Pink
- Pair of US 6 needles

GAUGE

26 sts and 24 rows = 4" over St-st.

Cast on 84 sts. Work 13" in St-st. Bind off.

SUITCASE

MATERIALS
- 1 x 50g ball DMC Natura Just Cotton (fingering/4ply 100% cotton; 50g/169yds) in each of shades N78 Lin (MC) and N41 Siena (CC)
- Pair of US 3 needles
- 2 x US 3 dpns
- Pieces of sturdy cardboard cut to following sizes:

Front & Back: each 4 ³/₄" x 3 ³/₄"
Top & Base: each 4 ³/₄" x 1 ¹/₂"
Two Sides: each 1 ³/₄" x 3 ³/₄"

GAUGE

40 sts & 40 rows = 4" over twist st patt.

TOP & BASE (both alike)
With CC and straight needles, cast on 40 sts. Work 2 rows in seed-st.
Work in patt as follows, using a separate length of CC for each border:
Row 1 (RS): With CC, k1, p1, * with MC, take right-hand needle behind first st on left-hand needle, k second st tbl then k first st; rep from * to last 2 sts, with CC, k1, p1.
Row 2: With CC, p1, k1, * with MC, p second st then p first st; rep from * to last 3 sts, p1, change to CC, p1, k1.
These 2 rows form twist st patt (MC) and seed-st borders (CC). Rep these 2 rows until work measures 3 ¹/₂". Cut off MC. With CC, work 2 rows in seed-st. Bind off.

SIDES (made in one piece)
With MC and straight needles, cast on 9 sts. Work 14" in seed-st. Bind off.

FINISHING
Press pieces lightly on WS using a warm iron over a damp cloth. Make cardboard inner by taping Base, Front, Top, and Back together to form a ring, then taping the Sides onto the main frame to form a box. Press fabric pieces lightly on WS using a warm iron over a damp cloth. Sew cast-on and bound-off edges of suitcase sides to make a ring. Fit sides around cardboard inner. With CC, sew top and base to sides using a neat, even blanket stitch.

Handle: With CC and dpns, cast on 4 sts and work a 2" length of I-cord (see p. 109). Bind off. Sew onto top of suitcase (see illus).

Straps (make 2): Cut six 19 ¹/₂" strands of CC. Knot together at one end, divide into three groups of two and make a braid. Stretch braid around suitcase 1 ³/₄" from edge. Secure at bottom of suitcase.

TELEPHONE

MATERIALS

- 1 x 50g ball Bergère de France Coton Fifty (fingering/4ply 50% cotton/50% acrylic; 50g/153yds) in shade 22493 Coco
- Pair of US 3 needles
- Set of 4 x US 3 dpns
- Adhesive tape
- Toy stuffing
- Small pieces of red and white felt
- PVA or fabric glue
- Pieces of sturdy cardboard cut to following sizes:

Base: 1 ¾" x 1 ¾"
Back & Dialpad: 1 ¾" x 1 ½"
Top: 1 ¾" x ¾"
Front: 1 ¾" x ¾"

GAUGE

29 sts and 36 rows = 4" over St-st.

FRONT, TOP, BACK & BASE

(worked in one piece)
With straight needles, cast on 12 sts. Work 3 rows in St-st. K 1 row (foldline). Work 11 rows in St-st. K 1 row. Work 5 rows in St-st. K 1 row. Work 11 rows in St-st. K 1 row. Work 12 rows in St-st. Bind off.

SIDE 1

Cast on 12 sts. Work 4 rows in St-st.
Next row (RS): K to last 2 sts k2tog (11 sts).
Next row: P2tog, p to end (10 sts).
** Rep these 2 rows twice more (6 sts). Work 6 rows in St-st. Bind off.

SIDE 2

Cast on 12 sts. Work 4 rows in St-st.
Next row (RS): K2tog, k to end (11 sts).
Next row: P to last 2 sts, p2tog (10 sts).
Work as for Side 1 from **.

HANDSET

Cast on 1 st.
Row 1 (RS): (K1, p1, k1) into st (3 sts).
Row 2: P.
Row 3: (Kfb) 3 times (6 sts). Slip 2 sts onto each of 3 dpns. Place a marker at beg of rnd. Work in rnds from now on.
Rnd 4: K.
Rnd 5: (Kfb) 6 times (12 sts).
Rnd 6: K
Rnd 7: (Kfb, k1) 6 times (18 sts).
Rnd 8: P.
K 3 rnds.

Rnd 12: (K2tog, k4) 3 times (15 sts).
Rnd 13: K.
Rnd 14: (K2tog, k3) 3 times (12 sts).
Rnd 15: K.
Rnd 16: (K2tog, k2) 3 times (9 sts).
*** Slip 3 sts from needle 2 onto needle 1 and work on these 6 sts.
Next row: K5, w&t.
Next row: P4, w&t.
Next row: K3, w&t.
Next row: P2, w&t.
Next row: K3, working wrap into st, turn.
Next row: P4, turn.
Next row: K5, turn.
Next row: P6.
Slip last 3 sts back onto needle 2 and work in rnds again (9 sts).****
K 2 rnds.
Rnd 19: (Kfb, k2) 3 times (12 sts). Stuff lightly.
K 18 rnds.
Rnd 38: (K2tog k2) 3 times (9 sts). Stuff lightly.
Rep from *** to **** once more.
Rnd 39: (Kfb, k2) 3 times (12 sts).
Rnd 40: K.
Rnd 41: (Kfb, k3) 3 times (15 sts).
Rnd 42: K.
Rnd 43: (Kfb, k4) 3 times (18 sts).
K 3 rnds.
Rnd 47: P.
Rnd 48: (K2 tog, k1) 6 times (12 sts). Stuff lightly.
Rnd 49: K.
Rnd 50: (K2tog) 6 times (6 sts).
Rnd 51: K.

Rnd 52: (K2tog) 3 times (3 sts). Cut yarn, thread through rem sts and pull tight. Secure yarn end.

FINISHING

Make inner cardboard by taping Base, Front, Dialpad, Top, and Back together to form a ring. Press fabric pieces lightly on WS using a warm iron over a damp cloth. Sew cast-on and bound-off edges of main piece to form a ring. Fit around cardboard inner matching foldlines to corners. Oversew sides to main piece. Cut small squares of red and white felt and arrange evenly over front of phone to make dial buttons (see illus on left). Glue into place.

NEGLIGÉE

MATERIALS

- 1 x 50g ball Debbie Bliss Rialto Lace (laceweight 100% wool; 50g/426yds) in shade 005 Black
- Pair of US 3 needles
- 20" length of narrow white ribbon

GAUGE

32 sts and 40 rows = 4" over lace patt st.

SKIRT

Cast on 97 sts. Work 4 rows in seed-st.

Row 1 (RS): K1, *yo, k2tog, k3, yo, k1, yo, k3, skpo, yo, k1; rep from * to end.

Row 2 & foll WS rows: P.

Row 3: K2, * yo, k4tog, yo, k3; rep from * to last 6 sts, yo, k4tog, yo, k2.

Row 5: K1, * k1, k2tog, yo, k5, yo, skpo, k2; rep from * to end.

Row 7: K1, *k2tog, yo, k7, yo, skpo, k1; rep from * to end.

Row 9: K2tog, yo, k9, * yo, sl 1, k2tog, psso, yo, k9; rep from * to last 2 sts, yo, skpo.

Row 10: P.

These 10 rows form the patt. Rep these 10 patt rows 3 times more.

Next row: * K2tog; rep from * to last st, k1 (49 sts).

Next row: P2tog, p to end (48 sts).

Work 4 rows of k1, p1 rib.

Next row: K14, bind off 20 sts, k14.

Bra Cups & Straps

** Work on 14 sts only as follows:

Next row: P.

Next row: K2tog, k to last 2 sts, k2tog (12 sts).

Rep last 2 rows to 4 sts, ending with a WS row.

Next row: K2tog twice (2 sts). Work 4" in garter-st for strap. Bind off. With WS facing, rejoin to rem 14 sts and work as for first bra cup from **.

FINISHING

Press pieces lightly on WS using a warm iron over a damp cloth. Sew end of each strap to back ribbed top. Thread white ribbon evenly around ribbed waistband and tie ends in a bow.

Y FRONTS

MATERIALS

- 1 x 50g ball Bergère de France Coton Fifty (fingering/4ply 50% cotton/50% acrylic; 50g/153yds)in each of shades 21365 Nigelle (MC) and 22493 Coco (CC)
- Pair of US 3 needles
- Pair of US 2 needles

GAUGE

29 sts and 36 rows = 4" over St-st.

BACK & FRONT (both alike)

With MC and size 3 needles, work as for Swimming Trunks (see p. 62) to ** (38 sts).
Work 2 rows in St-st. Dec 1 st at each end of next and every foll alt row to 28 sts, ending with a WS row.
Change to CC and size 2 needles. K 1 row, dec 1 st at each end (26 sts).
Work 3 rows in k1, p1 rib.
Bind off.

FINISHING

Press pieces lightly on WS using a warm iron over a damp cloth. Sew sides and crotch seams. With CC, embroider a Y on front (see illus).

The Lotus Blossom

SPA HOT TUB

A nice, intimate position this one, and not too difficult to achieve. Named after the yoga posture of the same name, you both need to be comfortable with sitting down cross-legged. The intimacy arises from the fact that you are both facing each other and your limbs are intertwined, giving the desire for a much slower pace than some of the more fast and furious postures (or the ones which make you ask yourself the burning question "How much longer is my back going to hold out?").

Since you are both sitting down, it's not a strenuous position, so it would be a nice one to try out when you're both feeling relaxed. Treat yourselves to a weekend away from the muck and dirt of everyday life . . . he might even be persuaded to try a cleansing visit to a health spa in a snowy mountain resort! As you breathe in the pure, clean air, relaxing in your cozy bathrobes and slippers (courtesy of the top-notch resort of course), you relax next to the hot tub with a bottle of champagne and reflect on your day of pampering: massages, facials, leisurely swims—you could get used to this! Real life seems a world away. The sun is still out but you feel the chill so you cuddle closer for warmth and have a long, lingering kiss.

The Lotus Blossom consists of the gentleman sitting cross-legged on the floor or comfortable surface. The lady sits in his lap and wraps her legs around his body. To vary the position slightly, the lady can lie back and pull her legs up into the lotus position, while the gentleman kneels in front of her.

Just make sure you remove your cucumber slices first or they might slip down into an uncomfortable spot.

CHAMPAGNE BOTTLE

MATERIALS

- 1 x 25g ball Jamieson & Smith 2ply Jumper Weight (100% Shetland wool; 25g/125yds) in shade 034 green (A)
- 1 x 100g ball Patons 100% Cotton 4ply (fingering 100% cotton; 100g/359yds) in shade 1740 Yellow (B)
- Small amounts of Black (C) and White fingering/4ply yarn
- Set of 4 x US 3 dpns
- 1 ½" x 3" piece of thin cardboard
- Adhesive tape
- Toy stuffing

With A, cast on 1 st.
Next row (RS): (K1, p1, k1) into st (3 sts).
Next row: P.
Next row: (Kfb) 3 times (6 sts). Place 2 sts onto each of 3 dpns. Place a marker at beg of rnd. Work in rnds from now on.
Next rnd: P.
Next rnd: (Kfb) 6 times (12 sts).
Next rnd: K.
Next rnd: (Kfb, k1) 6 times (18 sts).
Next rnd: K.
Next rnd: P (forms base ridge). K every rnd until work measures 2" from base ridge row.
Roll the cardboard into a tube to fit inside bottle, securing with adhesive tape. Fold end into shape of top of bottle and secure with adhesive tape. Insert into bottle and stuff very lightly. You may need to adjust the shaping as the bottle is completed.
Next rnd: (K2tog, k4) 3 times (15 sts).
Next rnd: K.
Next rnd: (K2tog, k3) 3 times (12 sts).

Next rnd: (K2tog, k2) 3 times (9 sts).
With C, k 2 rnds.
With B, k 10 rnds.
Next rnd: Kfb into each st (18 sts). Adjust cardboard inner and stuff lightly.
K 3 rnds.
Next row: (K2tog) 9 times (9 sts).
Next row: (K2tog, k1) 3 times (6 sts).
Cut yarn, thread through rem sts and pull tight.

FINISHING

With white yarn, sew a small label using duplicate st (Swiss darning—see p. 109).

CHAMPAGNE BUCKET

MATERIALS

- 1 x 25g ball Anchor Artiste Metallic (superfineweight 80% viscose/20% polyester; 25g/109yds) in shade 301 silver
- Set of 4 x US 3 dpns

Special Abbreviation

MB—(k1, p1) 3 times into next st, turn; p6, turn; k6, turn; p6, turn; k2tog 3 times, turn; p3tog, turn.

NOTE: Use 2 strands of yarn held together.

BASE

With 2 strands of yarn, cast on 1 st.
Next row (RS): (K1, p1, k1) into st (3 sts).
Next row: P.
Next row: (Kfb) 3 times (6 sts). Place 2 sts onto each of 3 dpns. Place a marker at beg of rnd.

Work in rnds from now on.
Next rnd: P.
Next rnd: (Kfb) 6 times (12 sts).
Next rnd: K.
Next rnd: (Kfb, k1) 6 times (18 sts).
Next rnd: K.
Next rnd: (Kfb, k1) 9 times (27 sts).
Next rnd: K.
Bind off.

SIDES
With 2 strands of yarn, cast on 27 sts and place 9 sts onto each of 3 dpns. Place a marker at beg of rnd.
K 8 rnds.
Rnd 9: (K8, kfb) 3 times (30 sts).
K 5 rnds.
Rnd 15: (K9, kfb) 3 times (33 sts).**
K 3 rnds.
Rnd 19: K15, MB, k16, MB.
Rnd 20: (K10, kfb) 3 times (36 sts).
Rnd 21: P.

Rnd 22: K.
Rep last 2 rnds once more.
Rnd 25: P.
Bind off.

FINISHING
Spray base with starch and press lightly on WS using a warm iron over a damp cloth, making it as flat as possible. Sew base to bottom of sides and oversew.

DECK CHAIRS

MATERIALS
- 1 x 50g ball Stylecraft Classique Cotton DK (lightweight 100% cotton; 50g/201yds) in each of shades 3669 Nocturne or 3670 Saville (MC) and 3660 White (CC)
- Pair of US 5 needles
- 2 ¼ yds of ¼" square strip wood (found in hardware stores)
- Small hacksaw
- ½" fine nails
- Spray starch

CANVAS
With MC, cast on 65 sts. Work 2 rows in seed-st, then 4 rows in St-st. Cont in St-st in stripe patt of 6 rows CC, 6 rows MC, 6 rows CC.
With MC, work 4 rows in St-st, then 2 rows in seed-st. Bind off.

FINISHING
Press pieces lightly on WS using won over a damp cloth. Spray with starch and press lightly again. Cut strip wood into lengths according to diagram A, and use nails to assemble deck chair frame according to diagram B, taking care not to split the wood. Wrap ends of deck chair canvas around sections 2 and 3, and sew neatly on WS.

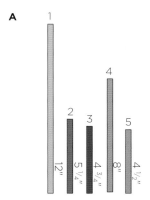

2 of each piece needed

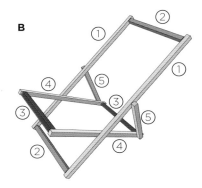

BATHROBES & SLIPPERS

MATERIALS

- 2 x 50g balls King Cole Cuddles Chunky (bulky 100% polyester; 50g 136yds) in shade #350 (White) (each bathrobe and set of slippers uses 1 ball)
- Pair US 10.5 needles (for His)
- Pair of US 8 needles (for Hers)
- 2 x US 8 dpns

BATHROBE (use US 10.5 needles for His and US 8 needles for Hers)

BACK

Cast on 17 sts. Work 9" in St-st. Bind off.

LEFT FRONT

Cast on 11 sts. Work 9" in St-st, ending with a WS row. (End with a RS row when working Right Front)
Bind off 5 sts at beg of next row (6 sts). Work 2" in St-st for back collar. Bind off.

RIGHT FRONT

Work as for Left Front.

SLEEVES

Cast on 13 sts. Work 6" in St-st. Bind off.

BELT

With 2 dpns, cast on 3 sts. Work a 16" length of I-cord. Bind off.

FINISHING

Sew shoulder seams. Sew the back collar edges together, and sew collar to back neck. Mark center of sleeve top and match to shoulder seam. Sew the sleeves to main garment. Sew side and sleeve seams. Fold sleeve ends to RS as cuffs.

SLIPPERS

With size 10.5 needles, cast on 3 sts. Work 8 rows in garter-st, inc 1 st at each end of 2nd row (5 sts). Dec 1 st each end of next row (3 sts). K 1 row. Bind off.

Straps

Cast on 3 sts. K 8 rows. Bind off. Sew straps to slipper base.

CUCUMBER SLICES

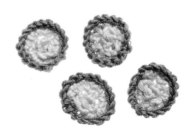

MATERIALS

- 1 x 50g ball Bergère de France Coton Fifty (fingering/4ply 50% cotton/50% acrylic; 50g/153yds) in each of shades 25307 Bourgeon (MC) and 20075 Herbage (CC).
  Only small amounts of each is used so any fingering/4ply yarn in two shades of green can be used instead.
- Set of 4 x US 3 needles

With MC, cast on 1 st.
Row 1: (k1, p1, k1) into st (3 sts). P 1 row. Place 1 st onto each of 3 dpns. Place a marker at beg of rnd. Work in rnds from now on.
Next rnd: (K1, p1, k1) into every st (9 sts).
Next rnd: K.
Next rnd: With CC, kfb into every st (18 sts).
Next rnd: With CC, k.
Bind off with CC.
Darn in ends.

The Bridge

ROOFTOP

This is another rather more adventurous position—made a little easier if the male partner is feeling particularly flexible and agile, and hasn't eaten a large meal previously. The Bridge is so called because of the shape the gentleman makes as he bends over backward—make sure he doesn't have a history of back problems, otherwise this might be a tricky one to explain away to the paramedics (or, more important, the neighbors.)

You might not want to go too far from home to try this one out—how about your own secluded rooftop garden overlooking the buzz of city life far below? Maybe you've just spent a relaxing summer's day tending to your patio plants and carrying out some light garden chores. As dusk settles you add the finishing touches to set the scene . . . fairy lights create a magical, intimate atmosphere. After a nice rest in your deck chairs to ease your gardeners' limbs, you decide this is the perfect spot to try out your yoga exercises. He stretches to show off his moves, and you look at each other as an idea comes to you both at the same time . . .

The position is achieved by the gentleman lying on his back on the floor, then pushing himself up onto all fours and arching his back. She sits gently (important to remember that word, otherwise he might cave in) on top of him with her feet on the floor taking the weight—she could experiment by facing different ways to find out which is best. This is a particularly good position for the lady's pleasure as she has control over the movement and direction.

Dare you take it to the bridge? Gives a whole new meaning to the phrase "I'll cross that bridge when I come to it."

LARGE PLANT

MATERIALS
- 1 x 50g ball DMC Natura Just Cotton (fingering/4ply 100% cotton; 50g/169yds) in shade N41 Siena (A)
- 1 x 50g ball Red Heart Margareta (sportweight 100% acrylic; 50g/281yds) in shade 01195 Green (B)
- 1 x 25g ball Rowan Fine Tweed (fingering/4ply 100% wool; 25g/98yds) in shade 360 Arncliffe (C) or small amount of light brown yarn for mud
- Set of 4 x US 3 dpns
- 6 ½" length of ¼" wooden dowel
- Small amount of floral foam such as Oasis
- Spray starch
- Thin cardboard
- Adhesive tape
- Toy stuffing

POT BASE
With 1 strand of A, work as for Milk Pail Base (see p. 42).

POT SIDES
With A and dpn, cast on 36 sts and place 12 sts on each dpn. Place a marker at beg of rnd.
Rnd 1 (RS): K.
P 2 rnds.
K 7 rnds.
Rnd 11: * K8, kfb; rep from * to end (40 sts).
Rnd 12: P.
K 7 rnds.
Rnd 20: * K9, kfb; rep from * to end (44 sts).
Rnd 21: P.
K 7 rnds.
P 3 rnds.
Bind off.

MUD
With C and 2 x dpn, cast on 1 st.
Row 1 (RS): (K1, p1, k1) into st (3 sts).
Row 2: P.
Row 3: Kfb into each st (6 sts).
Rnd 4: P.
Row 5: Kfb into each st (12 sts). Place 4 sts onto each of 3 dpn. Place a marker at beg of rnd. Work in rnds from now on.
Rnd 6: K.
Rnd 7: (Kfb, k1) 6 times (18 sts).
Rnd 8: K.
Rnd 9: (Kfb, k1) 9 times (27 sts).
Rnd 10: K.
Rnd 11: (Kfb, k2) 9 times (36 sts).
Rnd 12: K.
Rnd 13: (Kfb, k3) 9 times (45 sts).
Rnd 14: K.
Bind off.

FINISHING
Spray mud and pot base with starch and press lightly on WS using a warm iron over a damp cloth, making them as flat as possible. Sew base to bottom of sides and oversew. Cut a piece of cardboard 3" x 7". Roll cardboard into a cylinder, slightly wider at top than bottom, to fit inside pot (approx ½" shorter than pot). Use adhesive tape to hold shape together and insert into pot. Cut enough floral foam to stand firm in bottom of pot (approx 3" high). Use toy stuffing to lightly pad around foam, covering top. Sew mud into pot, approx ½" below top. With B, make a pom-pom (see p. 109) approx 4" in diameter, trim to shape. Push dowel into center of pom-pom, and carefully push other end through small hole in mud into floral foam.

SMALL PLANT

MATERIALS

- 1 x 50g ball Red Heart Baby (fingering/4ply 100% acrylic; 50g/207yds) in shade 08530 Brown (MC)
- 1 x 50g ball Red Heart Margareta (sportweight 100% acrylic; 50g/281yds) in shade 01178 Dulcet (CC)
- Small amounts of White and Pink yarn
- Set of 4 x US 3 dpns
- Toy stuffing
- Spray starch

POT BASE

With MC and using only 1 strand of yarn, work as for Champagne Bucket base (see p. 94).

POT SIDES

With MC and using only 1 strand of yarn, work as for Champagne Bucket (see p. 94) to ** (33 sts). Work 5 rows in seed-st. Bind off.

FINISHING

Spray pot base with starch and press lightly on WS using a warm iron over a damp cloth, making it as flat as possible. Sew base to bottom of sides and oversew. Stuff lightly, maintaining the pot's shape. With CC, make a pom-pom approx 2" in diameter, trim to shape. For a variegated effect, thread strands of white yarn through pom-pom, trim and fray ends. To make flowers, tie a knot in one end of a length of pink yarn, thread through pom-pom and pull through so flower sits evenly on pom-pom surface. Tie a knot in the other end to make another flower.

FAIRY LIGHTS

MATERIALS

- 1 x 50g ball Stylecraft Classique Cotton DK (lightweight 100% cotton; 50g/201yds) in each of preferred shades
- Pair of US 3 needles
- Set of 4 x US 3 dpns
- Stitch holder
- Fire retardant fabric spray

Petals (make 4)

With straight needles, cast on 1 st.

Row 1 (RS): (K1, p1, k1) into st (3 sts).

Row 2: Kfb, p1, kfb (5 sts).

Row 3: * P1, k1; rep from * to last st, p1.

Row 4: Kfb, k1, p1, k1, kfb (7 sts).

Row 5: * K1, p1; rep from * to last st, k1.

Rep row 5 twice more. Slip sts onto st-holder.

Flower Cup

Distribute sts from petals onto 3 dpns; 9 sts onto 2 needles, 10 sts onto third (28 sts). Place a marker at beg of rnd.

Rnd 1 (RS): K.

Rnd 2: * K1, k2tog; rep from * to last st, k1 (19 sts).

Rnd 3: K17, k2tog (18 sts).

Rnd 4: * K1, k2tog; rep from * to end (12 sts).

K 2 rnds.

Rnd 6: (K2tog) 6 times (6 sts).

Rnd 7: K.

Cut yarn, thread end through rem sts. Pull up loosely leaving a very small gap to insert light bulb and fasten off.

FINISHING

Weave any yarn ends to base of flower, use them to tie flowers onto fairy light cord. Apply fire retardant fabric spray.

EXTRA PATTERNS

TRIXIE'S KNITTING BAG

MATERIALS
For the bag:
- 1 x 50g ball Red Heart Miami (sportweight 100% cotton; 50g/131yds) in each of shades: 121 Black (MC) and 110 White (CC)
- Pair of US 3 needles
- 2 white pipe cleaners

BACK & FRONT (both alike)
With MC, cast on 20 sts.
Row 1 (RS): K1MC, * k1CC, k3MC; rep from * to last 3 sts, k1CC, k2MC.
Row 2: * P3CC, p1MC; rep from * to end.
Row 3: * K3CC, k1MC; rep from * to end.
Row 4: P1MC, * p1CC, p3MC; rep from * to last 3 sts, p1CC, p2MC.
Cut CC and with MC, work 3 rows in seed-st.
Next row: (K2tog) 10 times (10 sts).
Cut yarn, thread through rem sts, and pull up to gather slightly. Sew in yarn end.

FINISHING
Press pieces lightly on WS using a warm iron over a damp cloth. Sew sides and base of bag, leaving a small gap at top of sides. Wrap a length of black yarn around each pipe cleaner at even intervals (see illus). Twist a pipe cleaner into a ring for each handle, wrapping overlapping ends with black yarn. Sew handles to top of bag, with wrapped ends on inside of bag.

POPCORN

Used in The Perch, p. 64

MATERIALS

- 1 x 50g ball Bergère de France Coton Fifty (fingering/4ply 50%Cotton/50% Acrylic; 50g/153yds)in each of shades 22493 Coco (A), 23165 Ecarlate (B), and 23132 Cytise (C)
- Pair of US 3 needles
- Toy stuffing
- Thin cardboard
- Adhesive tape

SPECIAL ABBREVIATION

MB—(k1, p1) twice into next st, turn, p4, turn, k4, turn, p2tog twice, turn, k2tog.

CARTON

With A, cast on 40 sts. Work 2 rows in St-st. Join in B and work in stripe patt as follows:
Next row (RS): * (K1A, k1B) 4 times, k1A, p1A; rep from * to end.
Next row: * K1A, p1A, (p1B, p1A) 4 times; rep from * to end
These 2 rows form stripe patt, with 1 rev St-st at end of each patt rep to form corners.

Work 4 rows in stripe patt, ending with a WS row.
Next row (RS): * KfbA, patt 7 sts, kfbA, p1A; rep from * to end (48 sts).
Work 4 rows in stripe patt, working extra sts in A, ending with a RS row.
Next row (WS): * K1A, pfbA, p1A, patt 7 sts, p1A, pfbA; rep from * to end (56 sts).
Work 4 rows in stripe patt, working extra sts in A, ending with a WS row.
Next row (RS): * KfbA, k2A, patt 7 sts, k2A, kfb, p1; rep from * to end (64 sts).
Work 3 rows in stripe patt, working extra sts in A, ending with a WS row. Cont with A only as follows:
Next row (RS): * K15, p1; rep from * to end.
Next row: * K1, p15; rep from * to end.
Picot row: K1, * k2tog, yf; rep from * to last st, k1.
Work 3 rows in St-st. Bind off.

BASE

With A, cast on 10 sts. Work 1 ½" in garter-st. Bind off.

POPCORN

With C, cast on 17 sts. K 2 rows.
Row 1: K2, MB, * k3, MB; rep from * twice more, k2.
Row 2: K.
Row 3: K4 * MB, k3; rep from * twice more, k4.
Row 4: K.
Rep these 4 rows 4 times more. K 2 rows. Bind off.

FINISHING

Press pieces lightly on WS using a warm iron over a damp cloth.

Make an inner carton: cut out 4 pieces of cardboard by using the knitted fabric sides as a template, assemble into shape, and use adhesive tape to hold sides together. Fold upper edge of knitted carton to WS along picot row and oversew down. Sew side seam. Oversew base around bottom edge. Insert cardboard inner and stuff lightly so popcorn will puff out at top. Sew popcorn top to inner edge of carton along picot hem edge.

HIS SWEATER

Pattern chart to be used for His Sweater (The Indrani, p. 70), see p. 76.

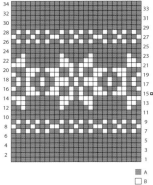

SHIRT

Used in The Erotic V, p. 28, and The Lustful Leg, p. 52.

MATERIALS

- 1 x 50g ball Bergère de France Coton Fifty (fingering/4ply 50% cotton/50% acrylic; 50g/153yds)in shade 22493 Coco
- Pair of US 3 needles
- 4 small white buttons

GAUGE

29 sts and 36 rows = 4″ over St-st.

BACK

Cast on 32 sts. Work 3 rows in St-st. K 1 row (hem foldline). Cont in St-st until work measures 2 1/2″ from hem foldline.

Armholes

Bind off 2 sts at beg of next 2 rows. Dec 1 st at each end of next row (26 sts). Work even until armhole measures 2 1/4″. Bind off.

RIGHT FRONT

Cast on 21 sts. Work 3 rows in St-st. K 1 row (hem foldline).
Next row (RS): P1, k1, p1, k to end.
Next row: P to last 2 sts, k1, p1.
These 2 rows form St-st and seed-st button band. Rep these 2 rows until work measures same as Back to armhole, ending with a RS row.

Armhole

Cast off 2 sts at beg of next row (19 sts).
Next row (RS): P1, k1, p1, k to last 2 sts, k2tog (18 sts).
Cont in St-st and seed-st band as established until armhole is 4 rows less than Back to shoulder, ending with a WS row.

Neck

Next row (RS): Bind off 6 sts, k to end (12 sts).
Next row: P to last 2 sts, p2tog (11 sts).
Next row: Bind off 3 sts, k to end (8 sts).
Next row: P. Bind off.
Place markers for 4 buttons, the first 3/4″ above hem foldline and next 3 spaced approx 1″ apart.

LEFT FRONT

Cast on 21 sts. Work 3 rows in St-st. K 1 row (hem foldline).
Next row (RS): K to last 3 sts, p1, k1, p1.
Next row: P1, k1, p to end.
These 2 rows form St-st and seed-st buttonhole band.
Rep these 2 rows until work measures 3/4″ from hem foldline, ending with a WS row.
Buttonhole row 1: K to last 3 sts, p1, bind off 1 st, p1.
Buttonhole row 2: P1, yrn, p to end.
Working buttonholes to match markers on Right Front, cont in St-st and seed-st band as established until work measures same as Back to armhole, ending with a WS row.

Armhole

Bind off 2 sts at beg of next row (19 sts).
Next row (WS): Patt to last 2 sts, p2tog (18 sts).
Cont in St-st and seed-st band as established until armhole is 4 rows less than Back to shoulder, ending with a RS row.
Next row: Bind off 6 sts, p to end (12 sts).
Next row: K to last 2 sts, k2tog (11 sts).
Next row: Bind off 3 sts, p to end (8 sts). K 1 row. Bind off.

SLEEVES

Cast on 18 sts. Work in St-st, inc 1 st each end of every foll 4th row to 28 sts. Work 4 rows.

Top

Bind off 2 sts at beg of next 2 rows (24 sts). Dec 1 st at each end of next and every foll alt row to 8 sts, then on every row to 4 sts. Bind off.

CUFFS (make 2)

Cast on 5 sts, work in St-st until work measures 3 1/2″. Bind off.

COLLAR

Cast on 5 sts, work in seed-st until work measures 5 3/4″. Bind off.

FINISHING

Press pieces lightly on WS using a warm iron over a damp cloth. Sew shoulder seams. Place center of sleeve tops to shoulder seam. Sew sleeves to main garment. Sew side and sleeve seams. Fold hems to WS and sew in place. Sew collar around neck. Sew the ends of the cuffs to form a ring and sew to bottom of sleeves, matching seams.

ABBREVIATIONS

alt	alternate		**p2tog**	purl two together
beg	beginning		**patt**	pattern
CC	contrasting color		**psso**	pass slipped stitch over
cm	centimeters		**rem**	remaining
cont	continue		**rep**	repeat
dec	decrease		**rev St-st**	reverse stocking stitch
dpn(s)	double-pointed needle(s)		**rnd(s)**	round(s)
foll	following		**RS**	right side
garter-st	garter stitch		**seed-st**	seed stitch
g	grams		**skpo**	slip one stitch, knit one stitch, pass slip stitch over
inc	increase			
k	knit		**sl**	slip
kfb	knit into front & back of next stitch (increases 1 st)		**sl 1**	slip one stitch
			sl st	slip stitch
k2tog	knit two together		**st(s)**	stitch(es)
m	meters		**St-st**	stocking stitch
m1L	make a stitch by inserting your left needle into the loop lying in front of the next stitch from front to back, then knit into the back of the stitch. Creates a "\" shape.		**st-holder**	stitch holder
			tbl	through back of loop
			tog	together
m1R	make a stitch by inserting your left needle into the loop lying in front of the next stitch from back to front, then knit into the front of the stitch (knitwise). Creates a '/' shape		**w&t**	wrap and turn (see Basic Techniques, p. 17)
			WS	wrong side
			yb	bring yarn to back of work
MC	main color		**yds**	yards
mm	millimeters		**yf**	bring yarn to front of work
p	purl		**yrn**	yarn round needle
pfb	purl one front & back			

EXTRA TECHNIQUES

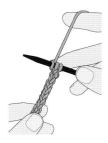

I-CORD

A knitted tubular cord, created with two dpns:
1. Cast on 3 or 4 sts according to pattern instructions.
Knit 1 row. Do not turn.
2. Slide sts along the dpn back to right hand tip of needle.
3. Swap needle to left hand ready for the next row. Knit the sts, pulling yarn tight across the back of the sts. Do not turn.
Rep steps 2-3 until cord is desired length.
Cut yarn, thread through sts and pull tight.

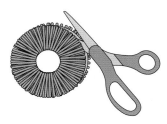

POM-POM

1. Cut two donut-shaped rings from stiff cardboard and hold together.
2. Wind yarn firmly around cardboard rings through the hole, until it is almost filled.
3. Using sharp scissors, cut yarn strands between the cardboard layers. Do not pull the layers apart.
4. Pass a length of yarn or strong sewing thread between the layers. Pull tight and knot securely.
5. Cut a slit in each cardboard ring from the edge to center hole. Remove cardboard and fluff out pom-pom.

FRENCH KNOT

Thread a sewing needle with one strand of yarn, or more for bigger knots.
1. Bring needle up at 1 and wrap thread once around needle.
2. Insert needle at 2, close to where it came up, holding wrapped thread taut.
3. Pass needle through the fabric, leaving the knot on the surface.
Do not to pull it too tight or the knot may disappear to the back of the fabric.

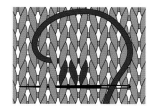

SWISS DARNING

1. Thread a blunt darning needle with yarn and secure at back of fabric.
2. Bring needle from back to front at base of stitch to be covered and draw yarn through. Insert needle behind the 2 loops of stitch above from right to left and draw yarn through. Insert needle into base of stitch again and bring up at base of next stitch to be covered.
Draw yarn through loosely so sts lie on top of knitting. Continue in this way until entire motif is embroidered.

INDEX

Acknowledgments

Eternal thanks as ever to Roger and Lucas for their amazing
support and for sharing me with my needles for endless hours.
To the lovely people at Rotovision for their humor, creativity,
and foresight, and to April for steely nerves when purveying the
concept. Special thanks to Wolfie for his photographic talents and
deadpannedness, and to Esther Richardson and Vanessa Hubbard
for helping me bring the characters to life.

Trixie
xoxo